CREWEL

EMBROIDERY

with texture and thread variations

CREWEL EMBROIDERY

with texture and thread variations

Audrey A. Francini

VAN NOSTRAND REINHOLD COMPANY
New York Cincinnati Toronto London Melbourne

ACKNOWLEDGMENTS

This book would never even have been started without the prodding and insistence of my many students throughout the entire country. I am grateful to them for their faith and for their ideas about the kind of material they want and need.

My thanks to Dorothy Calmes, who studied with Emma Pugh, director of the Wallingford Crewel Studio, Wallingford, Pennsylvania, for introducing me to the type of crewel described in this book, for teaching me some unusual variations on stitches, and for helping me to get started teaching crewel.

I also would like to thank my teacher Marianna Rossi Decker for her support and encouragement in developing the designs and color for the book.

My typist, Elaine Free; photographer, Loy Westberry; and editors, Nancy Green, Leslie Wenger, and Wendy Lochner, deserve my appreciation for their cooperation and tolerance in preparing the manuscript and photographs.

Last but not by any means least, I am grateful for the patience and understanding of my husband, who did not complain about skimpy meals, late washing, and an absent-minded wife.

All photographs by Loy Westberry unless otherwise credited
Designed by Loudan Enterprises

Published in 1979 by Van Nostrand Reinhold Company
A division of Litton Educational Publishing, Inc.
135 West 50th Street, New York, N.Y. 10020, U.S.A.

Van Nostrand Reinhold Limited
1410 Birchmount Road, Scarborough, Ontario M1P 2E7, Canada

Van Nostrand Reinhold Australia Pty. Limited
17 Queen Street, Mitcham, Victoria 3132, Australia

Van Nostrand Reinhold Company Limited
Molly Millars Lane, Wokingham, Berkshire, England

16   15   14   13   12   11   10   9   8   7   6   5   4   3   2

Library of Congress Cataloging in Publication Data

Francini, Audrey A
  Crewel embroidery.

  Bibliography: p.
  Includes index.
  1. Crewelwork.   I. Title.
TT778.C7F72   746.4'4   78-27160
ISBN 0-442-21651-3

The photo appearing on pages 6, 144, and 146 shows a sampler of filler stitches.

Contents

Introduction

Crewel embroidery, a type of needlework that is stitched in a two-ply worsted yarn, derives its name from the yarn itself. Although wool embroidery was worked in many European countries long ago and other forms of embroidery date back into early China, Coptic Egypt, and Greece, crewel embroidery as we know it today originated in England in the sixteenth century and was usually worked on a twilled fabric of cotton and linen. Its motifs were inspired by nature and represented familiar and unfamiliar, native and nonnative flowers, insects, and animals. The stitches that we use today were well established by the sixteenth and seventeenth centuries—since that time we have added numerous variations.

Any piece of embroidery worked in crewel yarn can be considered as traditional crewel embroidery. As often happens, the meaning of a word may gradually change over a long period of time. This seems to be occurring with the word "crewel"—today we find a variety of threads being used rather than just crewel yarn. At the same time new terms have been introduced to describe many of the newer types of embroidery. "Surface stitchery" and "creative stitchery" are the most commonly used, though they usually refer to work done in heavier threads and do not always employ traditional crewel motifs.

In this book my aim is to present designs and stitchery reminiscent of the traditional embroideries found in museums and at the same time to incorporate more modern ideas. The book is not intended to be an encyclopedia of every stitch ever recorded but rather to present the stitches and variations that in my experience I have found to be most useful and interpretative and that offer a variety of textural effects. This does not mean that you or I or anyone should ever stop experimenting and exploring other stitch possibilities, for this is the challenge of embroidery and the means of growing in our art.

The book first describes the various materials needed, or the "tools of the trade," and gives the basic information for working with these tools. A stitch section offers one or more samplers for each stitch category, illustrating some ways in which these stitches can be worked into designs. Each stitch is clearly described and diagrammed, and many useful tips are given as well as some variations not found in other books. The chapter on soft shading details many aspects of this subject that are usually passed over lightly or omitted entirely. There are chapters on color and design to help you to learn to plan and place your colors and stitches and to start creating your own designs. Three additional samplers with progressing degrees of difficulty are offered in the design chapter, as well as information on transferring designs to fabric and washing and blocking directions.

I have tried to design this book so that it can be used by the novice as well as by those with varying degrees of experience and skill in crewel. If you are new to the world of crewel, take things slowly at first—get used to your tools and learn to feel comfortable with them. Using a piece of practice material or "doodling cloth," learn the basics and try out some of the stitches. Then move on to the chain-stitch, buttonhole, flat-stitch, knotted, filler, and weaving samplers. Leave the couching and laid-work sampler until you are ready for more advanced work. Even if you already know something about crewel, it is still a good idea to review the basics before moving on to the samplers and stitches. Depending on your particular desires and needs, progress to the color and design sections when you feel you are ready for this step.

Your knowledge of stitches and color and how you apply them are your means of communication with all who will see your work. Learn a variety of stitches that can create effects that other stitches cannot create, then use these stitches to best interpret your design and communicate your thoughts and ideas to others. Whatever your personal reasons for starting and pursuing this delightful and rewarding art of crewel, never lose sight of the most important factor, to have fun and to gain the satisfaction of creating something beautiful with your own two hands! I sincerely hope that through the use of this book you will come to love the truly delightful art of crewel embroidery as much as I have.

Tools of the Trade

FABRICS

In the past crewel has been traditionally worked on natural-color linen twill. This is a strong, hard-wearing fabric that is closely woven and has firm body. These are desirable characteristics for an embroidery fabric. Linen twill can now be obtained in both natural and oyster or off-white colors. The color you choose should be suitable for the use to which the article will be put. The more strongly twilled side of the fabric is the side you work on.

British satin is another good fabric with a slight sheen, good body, and firm weave. It has the added advantage of being available in a wide range of colors. It often shows hoop marks and is best worked on a rectangular frame.

There are numerous other linen weaves and fabrics that are satisfactory for crewel. One method of determining whether a fabric is adequate is to buy a small amount and to use it for practice work. In this way you can see for yourself which fabrics best suit your purpose. If a fabric is too lightweight or too loosely woven, the finished piece is likely to show puckering and thread separation where the stitches pass through the material. If for some specific reason you still wish to use this kind of fabric, a closely woven but lightweight backing can be basted to the ground fabric and the embroidery worked through both. If the finished article will need to be washed, be sure that both fabrics are preshrunk before using, since they may not have the same amount of shrinkage.

Whichever fabric you do elect to use, a good grade is a wise choice. Too much time and effort is put into a work of embroidery to waste it on inferior materials.

YARN AND OTHER FIBERS

Crewel yarn is a two-ply, twisted wool yarn. It comes in various weights from the very fine Medici yarn to the heavy Persian yarn, which is supplied in most commercial kits. Some crewel yarns are available in a very wide range of colors and values of each color. Many of these hues are lovely, subtle, and muted. Other brands do not have a broad selection of colors and values, a most important factor when stitching. It is frustrating to need a certain color or value for a particular area and to find that you cannot get it.

Other fibers or threads that can be used either alone or in conjunction with wool are mercerized floss, Perle cotton, crochet thread, string, silk, linen, and any others that seem suitable to the subject matter itself. If the article will be laundered, all materials must be colorfast.

The threads you use should be compatible with the fabric. A very heavy thread or yarn worked on a very fine fabric would not make a good combination. Experiment with all kinds of fibers, and for any particular work or part of a work use the thread that is most suitable and best represents the subject.

NEEDLES

Three types of needles are generally used in crewel embroidery, crewel, chenille, and tapestry. Crewel needles are longer and have a smaller eye than chenille needles, which feature long, easy-to-thread eyes. The shorter length of the chenille needle makes it easy to maneuver, and its point has a long, gradual taper, allowing it to slip easily through the fabric. The tapestry needle is blunt and is used for weaving stitches, as it does not split and snag the yarn.

The size of the needle should be selected according to the size of the yarn. The needle must prepare a large enough hole in the fabric so that the yarn will not be unduly worn as it is pulled through.

Crewel needles come in assorted packages with sizes #1 to #5 in one and #3 to #9 in another. The lower the number, the larger the needle. Size #4 or #5 is good for most crewel yarns. Chenille-needle assortments range from #18 to #22 in a package, the lower number again indicating the larger needle. Size #20 or #22 is good for crewel yarns. Tapestry needles are sized the same as chenille needles.

HOOPS AND FRAMES

The use of some type of adjustable hoop or frame will result in consistently neater, more even work with smoother tension than that stitched without a frame. There are a few exceptions to this rule, i.e., when working the Chinese knot, Basque stitch, coral knot, and scroll stitch. For these stitches the fabric can be left somewhat loose in the hoop or worked out of the hoop.

Whichever kind of hoop or frame you choose, it must be adjustable so that the fabric can be kept taut at all times. If the fabric is loose, you might as well not use the hoop. Hand-held hoops are available in sizes from 3″ (7.6cm) to about 10″ (25.3cm), with some made of wood and the newer ones of plastic. The depth of these frames also varies, and the deeper ones will hold the fabric more firmly.

All hoops should have an adjusting screw (1-1). The older hoops with no adjustment or with a simple spring on the outer ring are not satisfactory, as it is impossible to keep the fabric taut and to fit them over the embroidery. Hoops can be put over embroidered areas without harming them, but it is wise to exercise caution. If possible, put the edge that touches embroidery down before the part that does not touch embroidery. Bullion and French knots (individual) may be distorted. This can sometimes be avoided by using a different-size hoop, or they can be worked last.

The larger round hoops are often attached to a lap, sit-on, table, or floor stand (1-2, 1-3, 1-4). The rectangular frames have tapes attached to the bottom and top bars. The working fabric is sewn to these tapes. The side pieces are adjustable either by

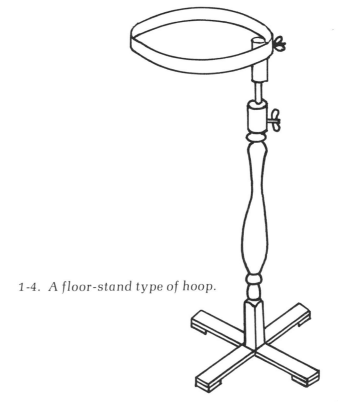

1-3. A hoop that clamps on a table.

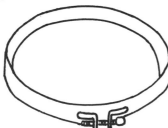

1-1. A round, hand-held wooden hoop with an adjusting screw.

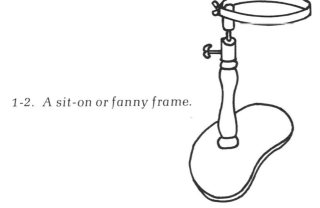

1-2. A sit-on or fanny frame.

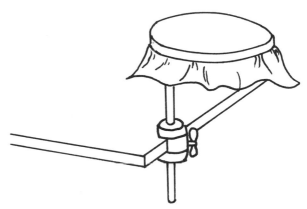

1-4. A floor-stand type of hoop.

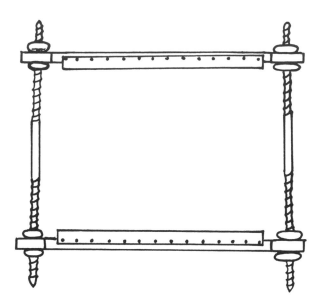

means of scored screw ends (1-5) or through a series of holes and cotter pins (1-6). On both these frames the sides are kept taut by lacing around the two side pieces. Another type of rectangular frame can be made by assembling artist's stretcher bars into the needed size. The fabric is then stretched and stapled to the frame, taking care to stretch with the grain of the fabric. If the fabric loosens, it can be removed and restretched. There are adjustable floor stands for holding these rectangular frames (1-7), or the frame can be rested against a table while working.

1-5. A rectangular frame that adjusts by means of screw threads cut into the side pieces.

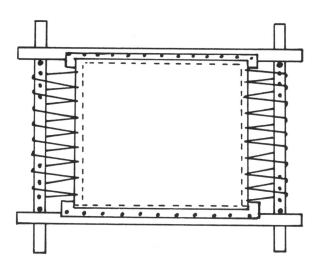

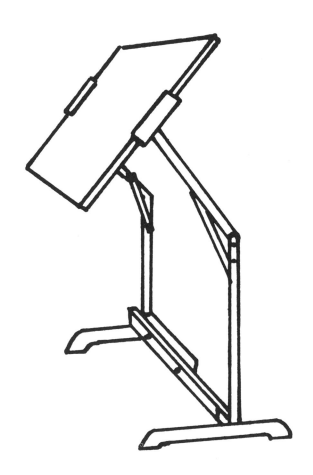

1-6. A rectangular frame with slat sides that adjusts by means of cotter pins and a series of holes. The lacing arrangement of the sides of the fabric can be used for this frame and the one shown in figure 1-5.

1-7. An adjustable floor stand for holding a rectangular frame.

MAGNIFYING GLASSES AND LAMPS

When working with floss, silk, or very fine wool threads, some people are more comfortable and experience less eyestrain if they use either a magnifying glass that hangs around the neck, magnifying glasses that clip onto their own eye-glasses, or a magnifying lamp. The latter comes in both table and floor models.

For the average person there is usually no need to use a magnifier when working with crewel yarns. If you do need to use one, first establish the size and spacing of the stitches without using the magnifier, then continue working, using the magnifier and keeping the same established size and spacing. This prevents making the stitches too small and avoids packing too many into a small space. Look at the work occasionally without the magnifying glass so that you get the overall effect of the stitching as it will be seen by others.

MISCELLANEOUS EQUIPMENT

You will need a pair of small, sharp-pointed scissors for cutting the yarn and for cutting out areas that need to be reworked (it does happen). Be careful not to cut the background fabric.

A thimble is not absolutely necessary when using the stab-stitching method except for tying in and tying off. But use one if you really feel the need for one.

A pair of tweezers is helpful for pulling out cut stitches when a portion of the stitching is being picked out.

A sharp, hard or medium-hard lead pencil is needed for marking guidelines on the fabric. It will not deposit too much graphite on the fabric or rub off on the yarn. You can also use an Eagle Veri-Thin sky-blue pencil (740½), which will wash out if it is not applied too heavily. Stretch-and-Sew sells a pen that marks with a blue line. It can also be used with very light pressure. With this pen be sure to thoroughly wet the embroidery with cold water only—no soap—until all the pen lines have completely disappeared; you can then proceed to wash the piece.

Using Your Tools

PUTTING FABRIC IN A ROUND HOOP

Place the area to be worked over the inner ring. Adjust the screw so that the outer ring fits snugly over the fabric and the inner ring; this may require several trials and adjustments. Push the outer ring partly down over the inner one; pull the fabric taut with the grain of the fabric; then push the outer ring the rest of the way down. If the adjustment is tight enough, the fabric will not slip. With delicate fabrics that might be marked by the hoops either use one of the rectangular-type frames or place tissue paper over the fabric before putting on the top ring and tear away the paper from the area to be worked. Always remove the hoops when you are not working.

FINDING THE NAP OF THE YARN

All wool yarn has a smooth and a rough nap. To determine this, pull a piece of yarn between the thumb and forefinger, using light pressure. Do this first in one direction, then in the other, using the same hand. Close your eyes and repeat the procedure. Another method is to pull the yarn between the fingers near the hand or to pull it across your cheek or just above your upper lip. Still another method is to hold the yarn against a good light. It will appear less fuzzy when stroked in one direction than in the opposite direction. It takes some practice to learn to feel the difference, but you will learn.

If the yarn feels smoother in the direction of the arrow (2-1), thread end A through the eye of the needle so that the yarn will be pulled through the fabric with the smooth nap. This prevents undue wear on the yarn and results in a less hairy appearance in the finished work. When working with a double strand of yarn, both pieces must run in the same direction. This means that you cannot use a long piece and fold it over in the eye of the needle.

THREADING THE NEEDLE

Follow these steps to thread the needle (2-2).

1. Fold an end of the yarn around the needle and hold tightly between the thumb and forefinger (1).

2. Pull the needle out, leaving the folded yarn between the fingers. This end should be just barely visible when the fingers are pressed tightly together. If you can't see it, the yarn is too far back (2).

3. With the eye of the needle flat, push it between the fingers over the folded end of the yarn, squeezing the fingers together at the same time (3).

4. Remove from between the fingers and pull through (4).

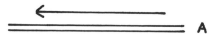

2-1. Finding the nap of the yarn and then end to thread through the needle.

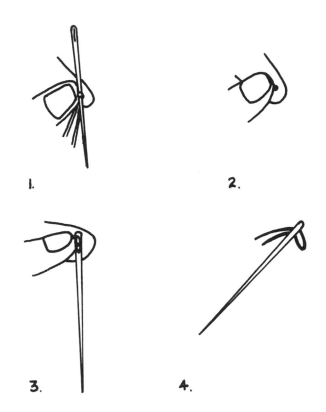

I.

2.

3.

4.

2-2. Steps for threading the needle.

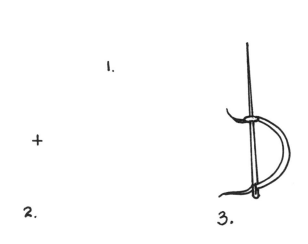

I.

+

2.

3.

2-3. Methods of tying in and tying of threads.

TYING IN AND TYING OFF

Never use a knot except perhaps for practice work. It may come undone or form undesirable lumps on the work when it is mounted. Follow these alternate procedures.

1. Take two or three tiny running stitches in an area to be covered by embroidery or directly on the working line, working toward the starting point and leaving a short tail. This is a good method to use with very taut fabric or when working a single line of stitching.

2. Make a tiny cross-stitch in an area to be covered by embroidery. If the yarn is heavy, this method sometimes leaves a slight lump.

3. From the back bring the needle halfway up through the fabric close to the starting point and in a spot that will be covered by embroidery. Turn the work over, remove the needle, and at the point where the needle was withdrawn take a tiny stitch, catching a couple of threads, pulling through, and leaving a short tail. Take another small stitch at a right angle to the first one, splitting the yarn of the first stitch as you make the second. This tie-in will hold firmly and lie flat. When a number of tie-ins are needed at about the same point, spread them around as much as possible so that a lump is not formed (2-3).

4. Threads may be ended with two or three running stitches or by method (3).

5. To tie off in an area completely covered by embroidery, use method (3), catching a little of the fabric as you do so. You can feel the resistance to the needle even though you cannot see it.

6. To tie off where there is a single line of stitching, take small stitches along the back of the line of stitching, again being sure to catch some of the fabric, not the yarn alone.

STITCHING

If you use a sewing stitch (2-4 [1]) with the fabric taut in a hoop, you will continually loosen and stretch the fabric as you push from underneath in order to make the stitch. You also cannot place the needle as accurately with the sewing stitch. The stab-stitching method gives the best results.

On any stitch in which the yarn is pulled completely through with each step, stab stitching is simple. But with stitches that are looped or linked together the procedure is a bit different.

Bring the needle up and pull through at the starting point. Put the needle down for the first step and pull through only far enough to allow the needle to enter the fabric for the second step (2). The yarn is then pulled all the way through, completing the stitch. With this method the needle can enter and emerge from the fabric in a vertical position, greatly increasing the accuracy of its placement. On the underside hold the yarn back, away from the point where the needle comes up, so as not to split it.

The tension on the yarn must be sufficient to result in smooth, neat stitching but not so great as to stretch the yarn. The latter will cause puckering. You must experiment and observe the results, and with practice you will get the feel of the proper tension.

Some stitches twist the yarn in one direction and some in the opposite direction. Observe which way the thread is twisting while stitching and give the needle a twist in the opposite direction between stitches. The only other means of compensating for the twisting is to occasionally let the yarn and needle dangle so that they untwist themselves.

Move the eye of the needle to a different spot on the yarn occasionally so that the yarn does not wear excessively at any one point. Use a piece of yarn no longer than 18" (45.5 cm). Too long a strand will wear thin, break, and be wasted. For some stitches such as bullion and French knots and any others that seem to cause excessive wear on the yarn, use a shorter piece.

Most stitches look better when worked with a single strand of yarn, even for the finer yarns. But others need the bulk and body of either a heavier single strand or double strands of a lighter-weight thread. Experimentation will indicate which is best with certain stitches.

When stitching, work just outside the lines so that no part of the line is visible when the stitching is completed.

When working with the lap, sit-on, floor, or rectangular frames, use both hands for stitching. A right-handed person would keep the right hand underneath and work with the left one on top. With practice a great deal of speed and accuracy can be developed with this method. For some stitches you will still need both hands on top, even with these frames.

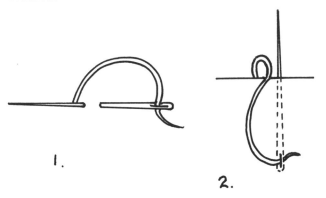

2-4. *The sewing stitch versus the stab stitch.*

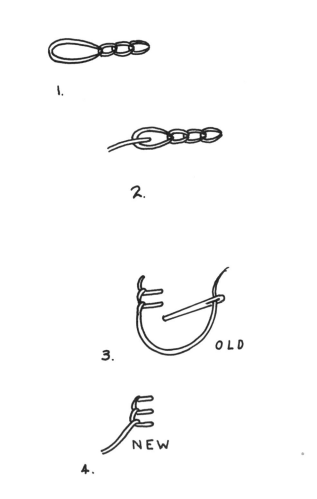

2-5. *Changing to a new thread in the middle of a line of chain, buttonhole, or any looped stitch.*

CHANGING THREAD IN MIDSTREAM

Changing yarn in the middle of any stitch that, in one of its steps, takes the yarn completely to the back presents no problem. The old thread is simply tied off at that point, and the new thread is brought up for the next step. This will cause no interruption in the pattern of the stitch. But with any of the looped or linked stitches the pattern will be broken by the tie-down stitch used to end the thread. For these stitches use the following method (2-5).

1. Using chain stitch as an example, take the old thread down for the beginning of the next stitch, leaving a loop on top (1).

2. Attach the new thread and bring it up for the second step of the same stitch (2).

3. Holding the new thread on top taut with the left hand, pull the old thread from underneath until the stitch looks the same as the previous ones. Tie off using two or three tiny running stitches and keeping the top side facing up. In this way you can watch the new stitch and make sure that it remains the same.

4. Changing thread with the buttonhole stitch is shown with the stitches separated slightly for the sake of clarity (3, 4).

The Stitches

Each stitch has a character all its own, producing an individual texture and pattern. These very characteristics of the various stitches can be used to interpret the design, to translate simple lines into beautiful stitchery, and to make the stitches work for you. How many stitches you know is not so important as that you know stitches that result in a variety of effects in your finished embroidery.

Make it a practice to always have a "doodling cloth" handy. Experiment with stitches, varying their size as well as their spacing and tension. Then try the same stitches with different types and sizes of thread. Observe how these various factors affect the appearance of the stitch. This kind of experimentation is a valuable tool when learning new stitches and even when perfecting the stitches you already know.

SAMPLERS

In this book the stitches are classified according to their basic structure—looped and linked stitches, flat stitches, knotted stitches, couching and laid stitches, filler stitches, weaving stitches, and shading (long-and-short) stitches.

For each stitch category there are one or more samplers worked mainly in the stitches included in that group, illustrating some ways in which they can be fitted into a design. There are obviously many other applications for each stitch, and every stitch described in the book is not included in the samplers. In a few instances stitches not belonging to a particular category are worked into a sampler if it seemed fitting and necessary.

The purpose of the stitch-group samplers is to help you learn to use the stitches and to adapt them to varying shapes. Learning the mechanics of stitches is actually only the first step. Learning to fit them into various areas and situations successfully is the next all-important step.

The samplers can be used for practice in working the various stitches and their variations. Or you can pick out any of the same designs, plan your own colors, and use a variety of stitches from other categories. Let your past experience in crewel and your individual needs dictate how you use the designs.

The samplers were worked mainly in Appleton crewel yarn, which is finer than most and comes in a wide range of colors and values. It is soft and blends better than most yarns, giving results impossible with other yarns. But if you are unable to obtain Appleton or wish to use some other yarn, the same designs and stitches can be used. The designs can also be enlarged or reduced as illustrated in the chapter on design.

Each sampler contains a key showing the stitches and colors used. The stitches are numbered consecutively throughout the entire book and are identified on the direction sheet by the appropriate numbers, which are underlined. Letters followed by numbers refer to the color key, with the lowest number indicating the lightest value. If a particular sequence in working various areas of the design is important or if further instructions seem advisable, these suggestions are listed after the direction sheet. Here are some suggestions for following the stitch diagrams.

1. First note the direction in which the stitch is worked.

2. Turn the diagram or your work so that both are properly oriented. Left-handed stitchers should turn the diagrams upside down. Some stitches can be worked either horizontally or vertically. One way must be selected for diagramming. Work in whichever direction is most comfortable for you, but be sure to turn the diagram accordingly.

3. Loop or place the yarn in the same position as in the diagram.

4. Note where the needle goes into the fabric in relation to the working line and to the last stitch.

5. Note whether the needle goes over or under the yarn.

6. Follow the directions in regard to the degree of tension on the yarn and the spacing of the stitches.

7. Stop after completing each step and check to see if your work looks like the diagram.

8. Keep in mind that stitches appear to be spaced apart in the diagrams. If this were not done, lines would run together, making the diagrams incomprehensible. The yarn is shortened in the interest of space. The diagrams also often show the sewing stitch for clarity, but use the stab stitch instead unless otherwise indicated.

PLANNING STITCHES

When planning stitches for a particular motif or for an entire design, consider the following points.

1. Does the motif itself suggest a particular stitch? This sometimes happens, particularly when the motif represents a specific object, and that stitch often is the right stitch to use.

2. Do you want a smooth, flat effect or a textured, raised appearance? Which stitches do you know that will give the desired effect?

3. Once you have decided on a stitch, look at the shape to see if the chosen stitch can be easily worked into that shape.

4. Plan stitches for an entire design before starting to stitch. This practice will ensure that textures and stitches will be balanced throughout the design.

5. Don't use every stitch you know in a single piece of embroidery. This would be like wearing all your jewelry at once. Simplicity has a charm all its own, and it is better to lean in this direction than to overdo the variety of stitches.

6. Consider the sequence in which the various parts of the motif need to be worked. The portions that lie underneath other parts should be worked first. This guarantees that the top portions will cover the underlying areas. These parts can be raised by padding the edges with split stitch, thus making them appear to be in front.

7. Be consistent in your treatment of a grouping of similar leaves or several flowers that represent a specific type.

3-1. Sampler illustrating the use of the chain
stitch and many of its variations, worked on linen
twill with Appleton yarn.

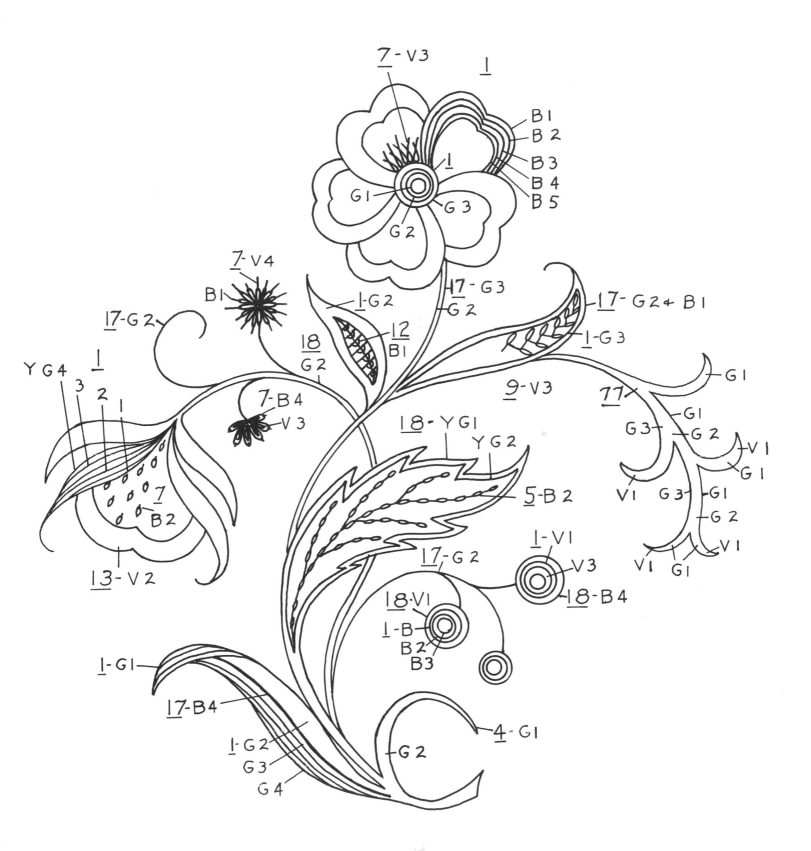

3-2. Line drawing and guide for the chain-stitch sampler.

1. Chain Stitch

The chain stitch is one of the most useful stitches that we have at our disposal as embroiderers. When worked with a fine wool, short stitches, and a reasonably tight tension, the effect will be totally different from that resulting from the use of a heavy yarn, larger stitches, and a loose tension. There are innumerable variations of the chain stitch, the most useful of which—in my personal experience—are included in this book (3-3).

a. Working from right to left (or from top to bottom; left-handed work from left to right), come up at A; loop yarn up and to the left, then down and to the right; and, holding this loop under the left thumb, go down again at A. Come up at B, bringing the needle over the looped yarn (1). When most of the yarn has been pulled through, hold it in an almost vertical position to the fabric and continue pulling the remainder through, keeping a firm but gentle tension and gradually bringing the yarn

Color Key
B 1, 2, 3, 4, 5—blue wool
V 1, 2, 3, 4—violet wool
G 1, 2, 3, 4—green wool
YG 1, 2, 3, 4—yellow-green wool
The lowest number indicates the lightest value.

Stitch key
1 chain stitch
4 broad chain stitch
5 cable chain stitch
7 detached chain stitch and
detached twisted chain stitch
9 feathered chain stitch
12 raised chain stitch
13 rosette chain stitch
17 whipped chain stitch
18 twisted chain stitch
77 split stitch

1. Top motif—all petals—work outer line of chain first in lightest value, then the others in sequence directly next to each other. Work center of flower in chain in a circular pattern. Then work twisted detached chain beginning in center of the open area of each petal, working first to one side, then to the other side, from the center out.

2. Leaf below top motif, right—work whipped chain on outside first, making chain in G2 and whipping with B1, a row of chain inside it, then feathered chain down the center of the leaf.

3. On spray to the right of the same leaf—start at tip and work in split stitch. Work the other tips, merging their stitches into the stem.

4. Center left—work rosette chain with two strands of wool if fine yarn is used, then the leaves and the detached-chain filler, using a single strand of yarn. Follow the placement of values on the direction sheet, with all four leaves the same. Work two rows of twisted chain for the stem coming from this motif.

5. Large center leaf—work in twisted chain, starting at tip on top side of leaf, twisting chains to the left; tack down at the point; twist one or two stitches to the right for inside edge of the point; take yarn to back. Start again at outside of first point, again twisting to the left until you reach the inside of the next point. Repeat as for first point until you reach base of leaf. Work a second line of twisted chain inside the first. Reverse the twist for the bottom side of the leaf. Work cable chain for veins, doing center vein first, then side veins.

6. Lower right under large leaf—work chain in circles first, then twisted chain just outside them.

7. Lower left—work whipped chain down center of leaf in blue. Shade remainder of leaf with rows of chain, following the placement of values on the direction sheet. Work overturned tip of leaf in light, bright green.

8. Work the remaining motifs and stems according to the direction sheet. Work lower-right leaf in broad chain, starting at tip and using a single strand, then changing to two strands after about one-third of leaf is completed. This broadens the leaf as it nears the main stem.

down toward the fabric in the direction in which you are working. This method of pulling stitches helps to assure an even tension for your work (2). About ⅛″ (3 mm) is the longest stitch that should be used with Appleton yarn.

b. Loop yarn as for the first stitch, go down again at B inside the first chain, and come up at C, bringing the needle over the looped yarn (3). Pull through as described above. Continue, being careful to make stitches even in length and to maintain an even tension. Too much tension will cause puckering, while too loose a tension will result in unevenness. End by taking the thread down just outside the end of the last stitch (4).

c. When used to solidly fill a space, all lines of chain should run in the same direction; if the shape has an apex and a base, these lines should start at the base and go toward the tip. The outside lines should be continuous, while any partial lines should be contained within the shape (5). Partial lines are necessary when the shape being filled widens or narrows. When more than one partial line is used, they should never begin nor end at the same points as the previous lines.

d. If you are shading with rows of different values, work the two outside lines first, then work toward the center, placing partial rows between complete rows. As you work, you can see how much space is being used by a certain number of rows and how much space is left to be filled. In this way you can judge the points at which you should start a new value. These values must be used in sequence and should be relatively close to each other in tone. A banded appearance will result if the values vary too much.

e. When starting a partial line, make the first stitch lopsided so as to taper the beginning of the row of stitching (6). When ending a partial row, take a slightly longer tie-down, angling it toward and tucking it in under the previous row (7).

f. If the motif you are working has points, the stitches that end at either inside or outside points should be tacked down—that is, ended—as if they were your last stitch. A small stitch is taken on the back close to this point where it will not show, and the needle is brought up again at the point at which it went down. The next stitch can then be angled in the proper direction. This procedure will maintain sharp points on the motif (8). Rows worked on the inside of these rows do not need to be tacked down at points.

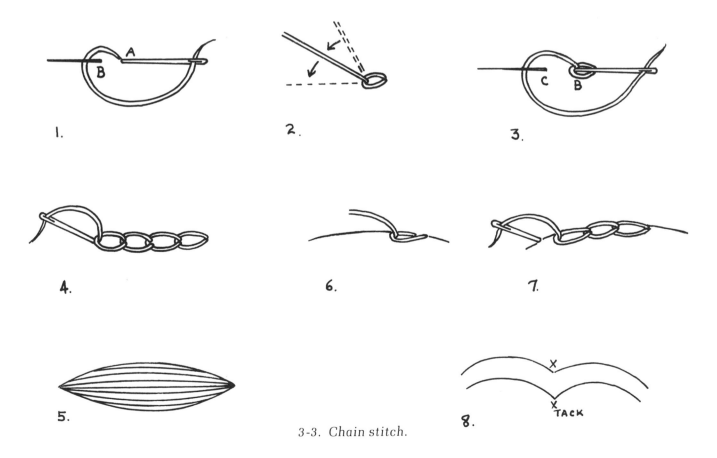

3-3. *Chain stitch.*

2. Back-stitched Chain Stitch
Make a row of back stitch (39) down the center of a line of chain stitch, using a contrasting color of the same type of thread or one of contrasting texture and sheen (3-4).

3. Basque Stitch
This is a braidlike stitch that is useful for decorative borders. It may be worked in straight lines or on curves. The spacing between and the depth of stitches must be adjusted to the weight of the yarn. Work from left to right. This stitch can be worked with a sewing stitch and without hoops if you wish (3-5).

a. Needle up at A, yarn up and to the right, needle down at B to right of A in front of the yarn. Needle up at C directly below B.

b. Carry the yarn from behind the needle, toward left and under the point of needle, left to right (1).

c. Tighten the yarn around the needle and pull through (2).

d. Needle down at D just below the loop and up at E between A and B (3).

3-4. Back-stitched chain stitch.

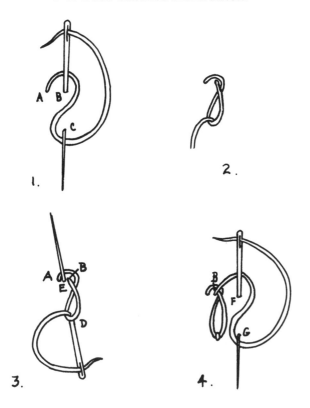

3-5. Basque stitch.

e. Pull through.

f. Needle down at F to the right of B and in front of the yarn, needle up at G below F. Twist yarn over the needle and back under the point as before (4). Tighten yarn around needle and pull through.

g. To work the stitch on taut fabric in a hoop, place the yarn in position (1), put the needle down at B, bring it up at C, then pull through. The needle can then be taken down at D and up at E (3).

4. Broad or Heavy Chain Stitch
Here is how to make a broad or heavy chain stitch (3-6).

a. Make small vertical stitch AB, working from top to bottom.

b. Needle up at C below B, slip needle behind AB, not catching fabric (1).

c. Needle down at C again (2).

d. Needle up at D below C (3), slip behind AB a second time and down at D again (4).

e. Needle up at E, slip behind the two first stitches, then down at E again (5, 6).

f. Continue, repeating the above steps and always slipping the needle behind the two previous stitches. End by bringing the needle up just barely below the last stitch, slipping behind the last two stitches, then down again where the thread came up.

g. The resulting heavy line of stitching is useful as a border, wide stem, or edging for a motif. Use the broad chain where a wide, heavy line effect is needed.

5. Cable Chain Stitch
In situations where a less solid line is desired, the cable chain offers a pleasing variation (3-7).

a. Needle up at A. Hold needle in front of yarn (1).

b. Twist needle up behind, then over the top of the yarn, bringing needle toward yourself, then down under yarn again (2).

c. Needle down at B and up at C, with the point of the needle coming over the looped yarn (3). Distance BC is the length of the chain itself, AB the length of the connecting stitch.

d. Pull through (4).

e. Repeat the twist of the yarn around the needle, then down at D and up at E for next stitch (5).

f. Pull through, bringing needle over the looped yarn—(6) shows several completed stitches.

g. Spacing may be varied to change the length of the chain or of the connecting stitch. The cable chain can be worked in a zigzag pattern (7), resulting in the zigzag cable-chain stitch. Two rows with French knots are shown in (8).

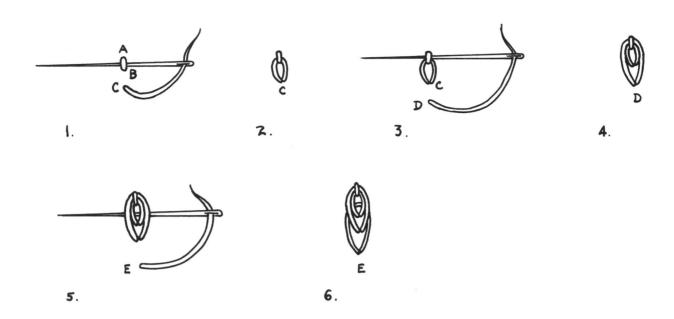

3-6. *Broad or heavy chain stitch.*

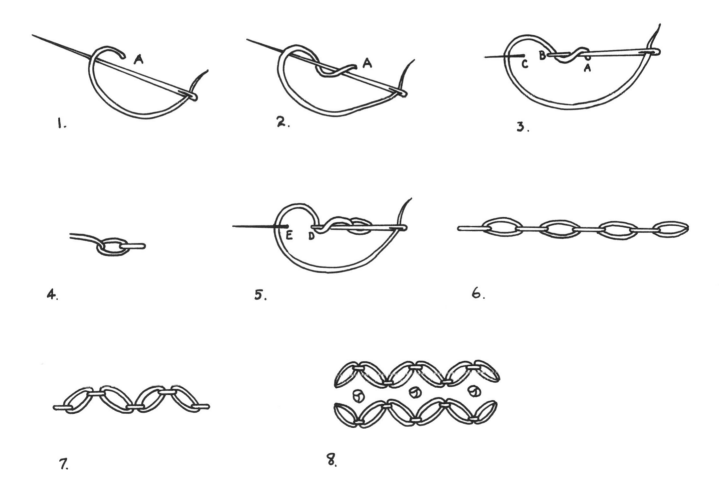

3-7. *Cable chain stitch.*

23

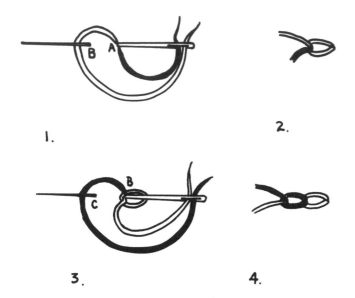

1.   2.

3.   4.

3-8. Checkered chain (magic chain) stitch.

6. Checkered Chain (Magic Chain) Stitch

This variation of the chain is worked with two strands of contrasting yarn in the needle. It can be used to create unusual effects or to simulate some degree of shading on stems (3-8).

a. Needle up at A. Hold one strand of yarn to the left in the usual position to make a chain and the other strand to the right, out of the way. Take needle back down at A and up at B (1).

b. Pull each strand through separately (2).

c. Reverse the position of the strands. Take the needle down at B again inside the last chain and up at C (3).

d. Pull through (4).

e. Continue, alternating the two strands as each chain is made.

7. Detached and Detached Twisted Chain Stitch

The detached chain (3-9) is simply an isolated, individual chain stitch, as opposed to being worked in a line (1). It may be used as a scattered filler or to form small flowers or small leaves (2, 3, 4). If a small leaf seems a bit too big for one detached chain, make the first stitch and fit a smaller detached chain inside the first one (5). A detached chain stitch nestled into a fly stitch, often referred to as a slipped detached chain, is an attractive variation as a scattered filler (6). Twisted detached chains can be used in the same manner (7).

8. Double Chain Stitch

A line of double chain produces ·an open, lacy border. The spaces can be filled with French knots or some other small, detached stitch if desired. Work between two lines from right to left (3-10).

a. Needle up at A on the upper line. Loop the yarn as for a regular chain. Needle down at B on the lower line and up at C on the lower line (1).

b. Pull through (2).

c. Loop yarn, needle down at A again, up at D on the upper line (3).

d. Pull through, loop yarn, needle down at C, up at E (4).

e. Continue, alternating sides.

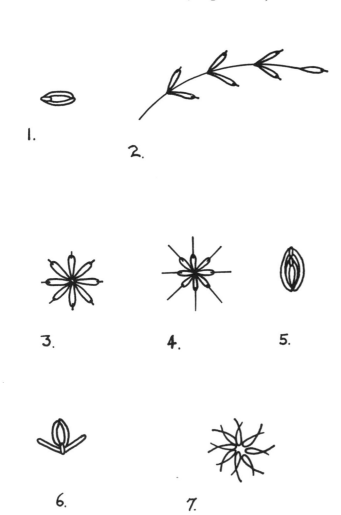

1.

2.

3.   4.   5.

6.   7.

3-9. Detached chain stitch.

24

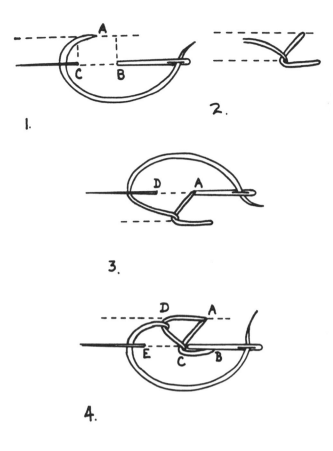

1.

2.

3.

4.

3-10. Double chain stitch.

9. Feathered Chain Stitch

This stitch is also called the chain feather stitch and the long-armed zigzag (3-11).

a. Make a slanting chain stitch, needle up at A, loop yarn, down at A again, up at B (1).

b. Pull through, needle down at C, making a longer than normal tie-down and keeping same slant as that of the chain (1).

c. Slant the next chain diagonally opposite the first one. Needle up at D directly opposite B, loop yarn, needle down again at D, up at E.

d. Pull through, needle down at F for tie-down, again continuing slant of chain (2).

e. Continue, alternating the slant of the chains and keeping the size of the stitches the same.

f. The stitches and the tie-downs must form a regular zigzag pattern. The length of the tie-down stitches can be changed to vary the effect, but you must be consistent once the pattern is established (3, 4).

10. Hungarian Braid

This is a variation of the broad chain stitch (4), but it produces a different pattern (3-12).

a. Begin as for the broad chain (1).

b. Instead of slipping needle behind the two stitches go behind the last stitch only (2).

c. It is easier to get under this stitch if the needle is slipped under before the previous stitch is completely pulled through.

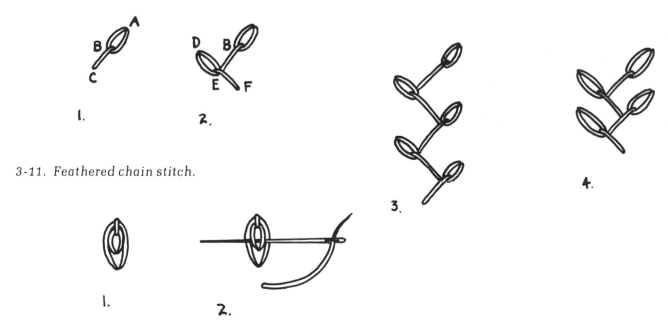

1.

2.

3.

4.

3-11. Feathered chain stitch.

1.

2.

3-12. Hungarian braid stitch.

11. Open Chain Stitch

A ladder effect is produced by this variation of the chain stitch. The open spaces may be filled with a small, detached stitch if desired, or the stitch can be used to couch down several laid threads (3-13).

a. Work between two imaginary parallel lines. Needle up at A on the upper line, loop the yarn, needle down at B on the lower line, directly opposite A, and up at C on the upper line to the left of A (1).

b. Pull through, needle coming over looped yarn.

c. Needle down at D on the lower line and to left of B, up at E on upper line to left of C (2).

d. Pull through, needle coming over looped yarn.

e. Since points C and D are separated, they spread the ends of the chain apart. Space the stitches evenly and pull with an even tension.

12. Raised Chain (Band) Stitch

Raised chain stitch can be worked over horizontal crossbars, over the bars of a completed horizontal spider, or over the spokes of a circular whipped spider (provided that these spokes are reasonably close together). It may be worked in the same type of yarn but in a contrasting color; in Perle cotton, silk buttonhole twist, or any other type that gives the desired effect (3-14).

a. If the stitch is not being worked over a spider, lay evenly spaced bars about ⅛″ (3 mm) apart and ⅛″ wide (for a single line of raised chain) across space.

b. Needle up at A, top center of the shape.

c. Using a tapestry needle, slide it under the first bar at point B, no fabric, slanting from bottom center of this bar slightly to the left of center of top of same bar (1).

d. Pull through upwards, being careful not to pull the bar out of line (2).

e. Loop the yarn down and to the right. Slip the needle under the same bar, top to bottom at C, just to right of A, and slanting toward bottom center, no fabric (3).

f. Pull the needle through, coming over the looped yarn (4).

g. Repeat these two steps on the second bar (5, 6, 7).

h. When the first part of the second stitch is pulled through, it will hold the stitch above in place. Be sure to hold the yarn up on the first step and down on the second.

i. The horizontal bars can be made wider and several rows of raised chain worked side by side. When doing this, be careful not to crowd the rows together.

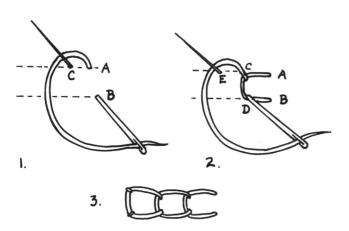

3-13. Open chain stitch.

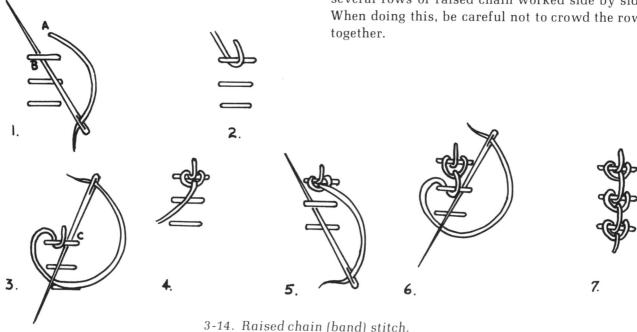

3-14. Raised chain (band) stitch.

13. Rosette Chain Stitch

The rosette chain stitch makes a beautiful braided edging. It works well on a straight line, on a curve, or in a small circle with the ends of the chain flaring out to form flower petals. Do not use on articles that will require frequent laundering or will be subjected to abrasion. Use a firm thread or double strands of a fine thread. Work from right to left (3-15).

a. Needle up at A, yarn looped down and slightly to the left, then to the right and up.

b. Needle down at B slightly to the left of A, up at C, needle slanting very slightly to the right, the point coming over the yarn (1).

c. Pull through. The result is a twisted chain.

d. Slip the needle, from bottom to top, under the yarn just to the left of point A, no fabric (2).

e. Pull through while holding the thumb or finger over stitch to prevent pulling too tightly.

f. Needle down at D, to the left of B, up at E, yarn passing in front of the needle at the top and under the point of the needle at the base (3).

g. Pull through, slip the needle under the yarn to the left of B (4).

h. Continue working toward the left, maintaining even tension on the yarn. On a curve the stitches will fan somewhat, depending on the tightness of the curve.

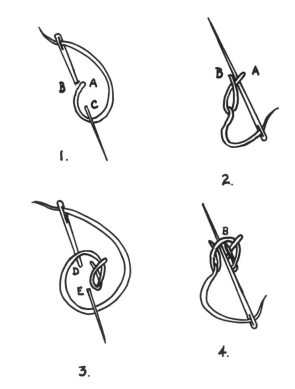

3-15. Rosette chain stitch.

14. Spine Stitch

The spine stitch can be worked with the spine portion extending to either side of the line of chain or with spines on alternate sides. It may be used simply as a line stitch, as an edging for a motif, or to make a spiny stem (3-16).

a. Make a regular chain stitch, needle up at A, loop yarn, down at A again, up at B, pulling through, needle coming over loop (1).

b. Needle down at C, about 2/3 the length of the chain and above it, and up at B inside the chain (2).

c. Pull through.

d. Needle down at B inside the last chain, loop yarn and up at D coming over the loop to form the second chain (3).

e. Needle down at E and up at D inside the second chain, forming the second spine (4).

f. Pull through—(5) shows the spine on the opposite side of the chain; (6) shows several consecutive stitches. Experiment with the yarn used for the best spacing and angle of the spine.

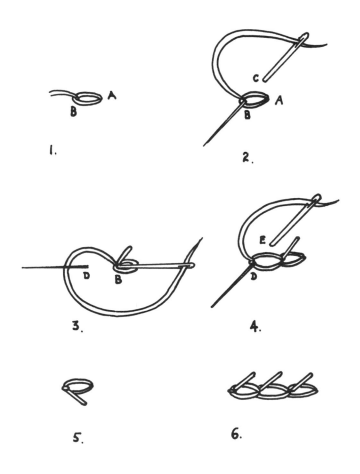

3-16. Spine stitch.

15. Threaded Chain Stitch

Here is how to make the threaded chain stitch (3-17).

a. Make a line of chain stitch.

b. Using a thread of contrasting color—and contrasting texture and sheen if desired—thread by slipping the needle under one stitch in one direction, then back under next stitch in opposite direction. Do not go into fabric. Continue weaving back and forth under the stitches (1, 2).

c. At the end of row turn the work and weave back, with needle passing in the opposite direction when going under stitches (3).

d. Do not pull this lacing thread too tight; leave it slightly relaxed.

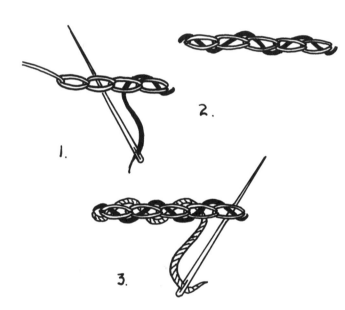

3-17. Threaded chain stitch.

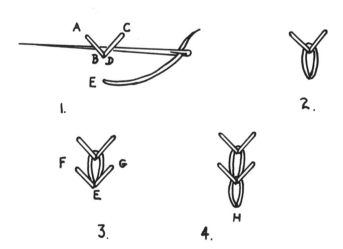

3-18. Wheat-ear stitch.

16. Wheat-ear Stitch

This stitch may be worked as a detached stitch, scattered in an area as a filler, or used in a continuous line (3-18).

a. Make two slanting stitches AB and CD.

b. Needle up at E, slip the needle behind the base of the two slanted stitches, no fabric (1).

c. Pull through, needle down at E again (2).

d. Make two more slanted stitches, FE and GE (3).

e. Needle up at H, slip behind the base of the last pair of slanted stitches, down at H again (4).

f. Continue, making the slant and length of stitches consistent.

17. Whipped Chain Stitch

If a row of chain stitch is to be whipped, do not make the stitches too small—no less than about ⅛" (3 mm) with Appleton yarn—and do not use a loose tension (3-19).

a. Slip the needle under both threads of first chain, no fabric, keeping yarn away from direction of whipping (1).

b. Pull through, carry the yarn over the top of the stitching, and slip the needle under the second chain from the same side (2).

c. Repeat for the third chain, then pull gently but firmly on the yarn until whipped stitches are smooth.

d. Continue to the end of the row, with the needle always going under the stitches from the same side and pulling smooth about every third stitch.

18. Twisted Chain Stitch

The twisted chain stitch produces a textured line. It can also appear spiny, depending on the placement of the needle in the second step of the procedure. The effect of this stitch, however, is different from that of the spine stitch. The twist can be placed on either side of the row of chain; rows may be placed side by side with projecting portions all to one side, or two rows may be placed next to each other with projections to opposing sides (3-20).

a. Needle up at A, loop the yarn, needle down at B above and slightly to right of A, and up at C in line with and to the left of A (1).

b. Pull through, bringing the needle over the looped yarn (2).

c. Needle down at D, above and slightly to the right of C (3) and up at E, pull through—(4, 5) show the twist to the opposite side.

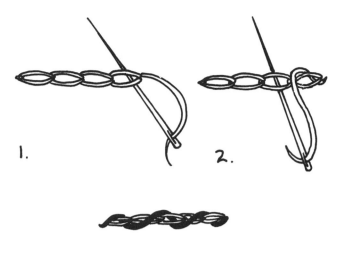

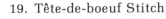

I.   **2.**

3.

3-19. Whipped chain stitch.

19. Tête-de-boeuf Stitch

Here is how to make the tête-de-boeuf stitch (3-21).

   a. Needle up at A, down at B, and up at C, making the beginning of a fly stitch (1).

   b. Needle back down at C, yarn looped down and to the right, needle up at D (2).

   c. Pull through, needle coming over looped yarn, making a chain stitch.

   d. Needle down at E for tie-down (3).

   This stitch may be used as a scattered filler or in rows with the horns touching.

20. Zigzag Chain Stitch

Make the individual chain stitches as for the regular chain stitch but angle the stitches alternately in opposing directions (3-22). Various patterns can be produced with several rows of zigzag chain stitch. It can be used on curves as well as on straight lines.

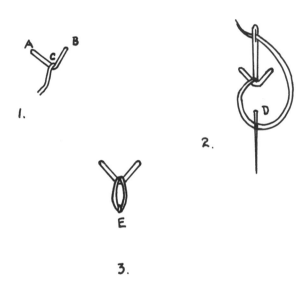

3-21. Tête-de-boeuf stitch.

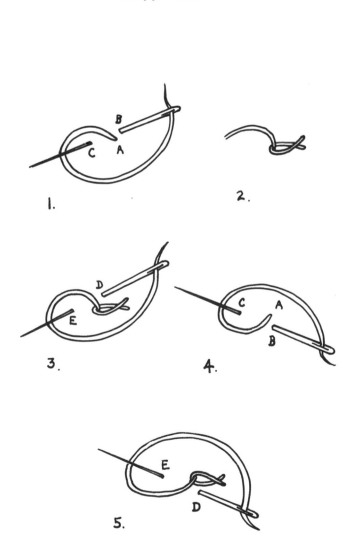

3-20. Twisted chain stitch.

3-22. Zigzag chain stitch.

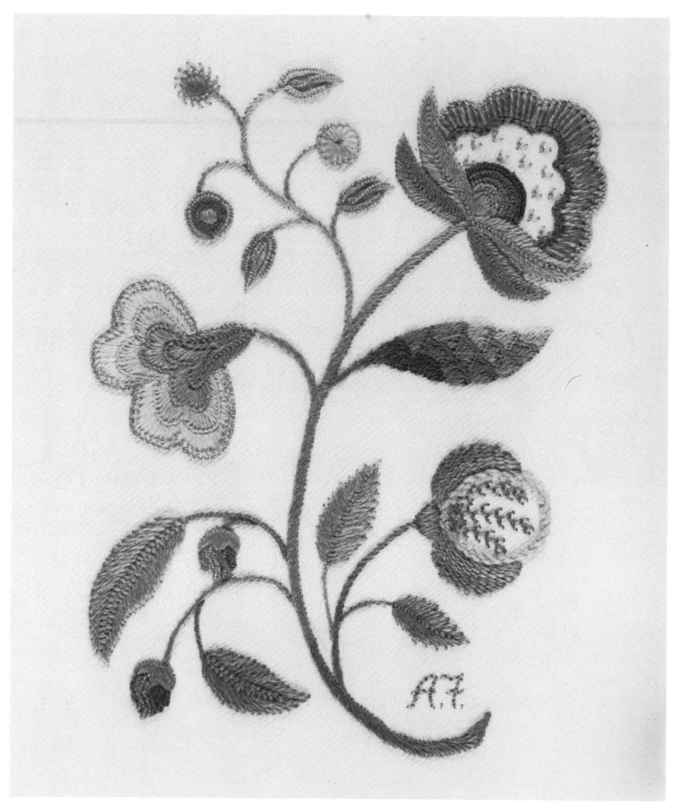

3-23. Sampler illustrating the buttonhole stitch,
many of its variations, and other looped stitches,
worked on linen twill in Appleton yarn.

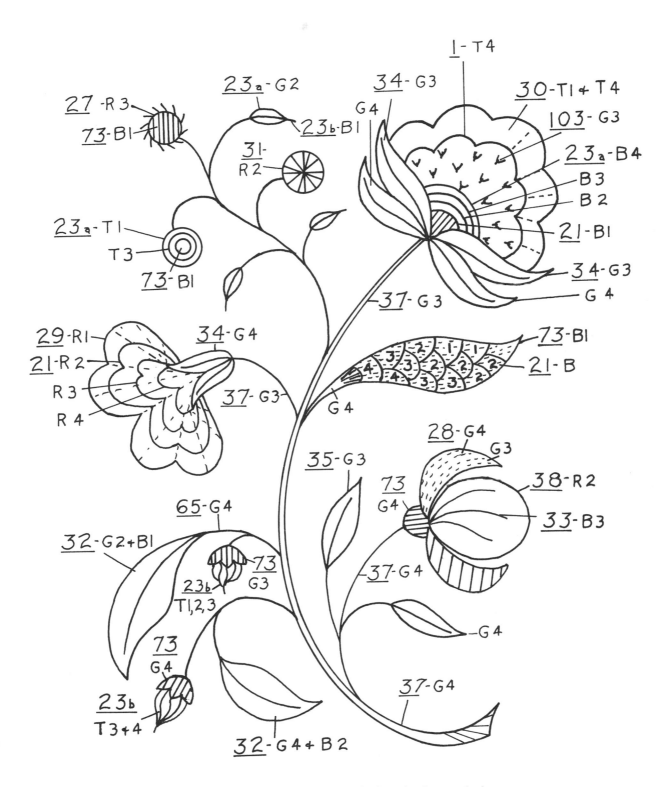

3-24. Line drawing and guide for the buttonhole-stitch sampler.

Color Key
R 1, 2, 3, 4—rose wool
T 1, 2, 3, 4—turquoise wool
B 1, 2, 3, 4—brown wool
G 2, 3, 4—green wool
The lowest number indicates the lightest value.

Stitch Key

1	chain stitch
21	close buttonhole stitch
23a	detached buttonhole bar
23b	twisted detached buttonhole bar
27	reverse buttonhole stitch
28	raised buttonhole stitch
29	tailor's buttonhole stitch
30	Wallingford stitch
31	wheel buttonhole stitch
32	Cretan stitch
33	feather stitch
34	closed fly stitch
35	serrated closed fly stitch
37	rope and narrow rope stitch
38	scroll stitch
73	satin stitch
65	whipped outline stitch
103	detached fly stitch

1. Upper-right motif—work the Wallingford stitch using a single strand of yarn and leaving space to be filled with one strand of darker yarn. Fill, then work one row of chain on the inner edge, tacking at points. Work leaves. Stitch the outside row of detached buttonhole arc in the darkest brown, then work the remaining rows in sequence. The center section is close buttonhole in the lightest value.

2. Brown leaf—work the tip in satin stitch. Then do the overlapping sections in close buttonhole, following the values marked on the direction sheet and working toward the base. Keep the direction of the stitches in line on all sections. Split into the base area with green stitches for the stem at different levels, as in shading. The buttonhole edges are on the heavy lines. Fill the outer sides with satin stitch as needed, keeping the spacing and direction the same.

3. Lower right—work raised buttonhole on lower section from the tip to the base, starting on inside curve. On the upper section you may work from bottom to top or from top to bottom, but in the latter case you must loop the yarn to the right or toward the center of the motif.

4. Small circles—upper left, work reverse buttonhole, then satin stitch inside it, padding if desired and slipping the needle out from under on one end and down under the buttonhole edge on the other side.

5. Lower left—work the outer circle of detached buttonhole first, then the inside, and fill with satin stitch.

6. Center left—work the outer row first, using tailor's buttonhole, then the next rows in sequence in close buttonhole. With dark rose wool or Perle work the buttonhole stitch over the ridge of the outer row, no fabric, making one stitch for each one of the base row and pulling back level with the fabric.

7. Leaves—work Cretan stitch with one strand of green and one of brown threaded in the needle together.

8. Rope stitch on stem—start at the base of the turquoise flower and change to a darker value about three-quarters the distance to the base. Watch the direction on the horizontal base portion, crowding the ends of the stitches on the inside edge as you swing around the outside edge. Blend the narrow rope stitch from the other stems gradually into the main stem.

21. Close Buttonhole Stitch

This stitch is often referred to as simply the buttonhole stitch and is worked with the individual stitches next to each other so that no fabric shows between them. It is a most versatile and useful stitch. It makes an effective border for a motif that has an open filler; this border may be narrow, medium, or wide, whichever scale fits the motif best. It can also be worked in consecutive bands to completely fill a leaf, flower, or motif. The stitch is worked from left to right, or from right to left for lefties (3-25).

a. Needle up at A on outside line. On the first stitch only, if it lies on the outside edge of the motif, needle down at B on inside line and up again at A, keeping yarn to the left (1). This puts a straight stitch on the outside edge, eliminating the slight hook of the usual buttonhole, and leaves yarn in correct position for next stitch.

b. Needle down at C just beside and to the right of B and up to D just to the right of A on the outside line, yarn looped down and to the right (2).

c. Pull through, coming over the looped yarn.

d. Repeat, placing stitches close together and keeping stitches perpendicular to inside and outside lines (3). If the shape is decidedly curved, you will find it helpful to mark perpendicular lines at intervals to serve as guides as you work. When the stitching reaches one of these lines, the stitches should line up with it. Since the inside curve is usually shorter than the outside curve, stitches will occasionally need to share the same hole on the inside line while the outside part of the stitch is placed alongside the last one. This enables you to change direction slightly, swinging around the curve and still keeping the stitches perpendicular. Change direction gradually and watch the guidelines as you approach them, judging how much compensation is necessary. If the area you are working has points, the stitch made at the point should be tacked down (4).

e. Take needle down just outside the stitch as if to end the line of stitching. Making a small tacking stitch on the back where it will not show, bring the needle up in the same hole in which it went down. Continue with the buttonhole. The purpose of this maneuver is to maintain sharp points and to prevent a rounding at that spot.

f. When working consecutive bands of buttonhole, do the outside band first. The ridge made by the successive bands of buttonhole will then overlay the inside edge of the previous band. It is important when working consecutive bands that the direction of the stitches in all bands be in line. Marking guidelines will help you accomplish this. By changing values of the color on the different bands you can achieve some degree of shading.

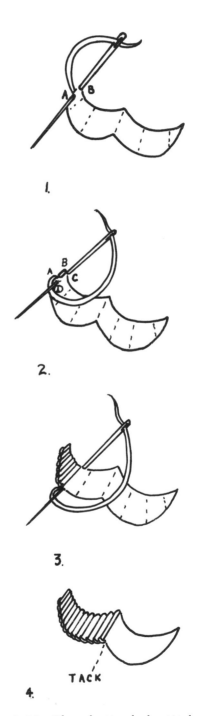

3-25. *Close buttonhole stitch.*

22. Closed Buttonhole Stitch

In this version of the buttonhole stitch the base of the stitch remains open while the ends are brought together. There are several ways in which this can be done to produce a variety of patterns. Two possibilities are shown here (3-26). Experiment to find some variations of your own.

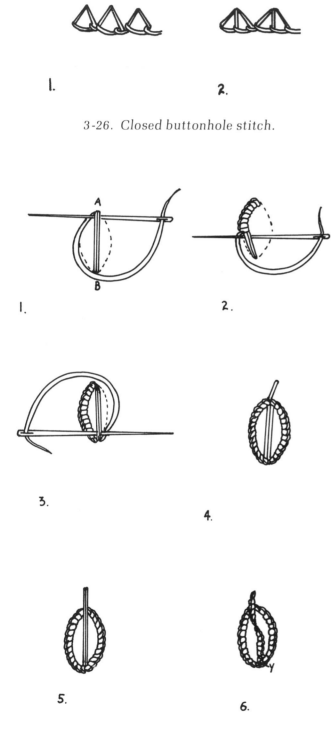

1.　　　　　　　2.

3-26. Closed buttonhole stitch.

1.　　　　　　　2.

3.　　　　　　　4.

5.　　　　　　　6.

3-27. Detached buttonhole bars.

23. Detached Buttonhole Bars

Detached buttonhole bars are worked over several stitches laid side by side and are attached to the fabric only at their ends and at occasional points to hold them in position.

Here is how to make a small leaf using detached buttonhole bars (3-27).

a. Lay two strands of yarn beside each other extending from the tip to the base AB (1).

b. Needle up at A at the tip, just outside the strands, work buttonhole around the strands of yarn, no fabric (1). Stitches should lie next to each other and be pulled with a firm, even tension so that resulting bar is smooth.

c. At the halfway point hold the bar along the leaf line (it will stretch enough if strands are not laid in too tightly), and, while making next buttonhole stitch, catch a few threads of fabric underneath where the bar will lie (2). This will hold the bar in place along the leaf line. Do not pull this stitch any tighter than the others.

d. Continue with the buttonhole stitch (no fabric) until the next to the last stitch. Again, catch a few threads of fabric as you make this stitch.

e. Make the last buttonhole stitch, take the needle down at the outside edge of the stitching, pull tightly, and tack on back.

f. Turn the work so that the unworked side of the leaf faces you and lay two more strands of yarn from the base to just barely inside the tip end of completed bar.

g. Continue working buttonhole from base to tip (3), tacking as on first side.

h. The center of the leaf may be finished by putting two straight stitches inside the leaf and a short, slightly angled stitch outside the tip—angle to continue curve of stem (4).

Here is how to make a twisted detached buttonhole bar.

a. An alternate method for finishing center is to lay two more strands of a contrasting color or value tightly from inside the base outside the tip slightly toward the left side (5). Start the buttonhole stitch a bit below the tip and use a firmer tension on the first two or three stitches. This helps to make a point on the outer end of this center bar. Do not tack at the middle but hold in place under the left thumb until the bar is filled.

b. Slip the point of needle under the inside edge of the right-hand bar at Y (6). This will tack the bar just made into a rolled-over or twisted position.

c. Small flower buds may be made with three, five, or seven of these twisted bars, working a long center bar, two slightly shorter ones on either side, and two still shorter ones on the outsides and shaping them into a bud shape (7).

Small circles can also be worked in this same stitch. Make an equilateral triangle within the circle, laying two or three strands of yarn along each side of the triangle (8).

a. Starting at one point of the triangle, work detached buttonhole, taking at the halfway point (x) with a buttonhole stitch that catches the fabric (9).

b. When end of one side is reached, make the next stitch through the fabric, covering point at which the two sides meet (10).

c. Without breaking the continuity of the buttonhole stitch, continue working the second and third sides, tacking with a buttonhole stitch at the middle of each side as well as at the points of the triangle.

d. To finish circle, take needle down just inside the ridge of the first buttonhole stitch made (11).

To make an arc or a series of concentric arcs, place a second needle at the center of the arc (12).

a. Needle up at A, carry the yarn behind the second needle, down at B. Repeat, laying two or three strands in all.

b. Needle up at A on the outside, work detached buttonhole over the strands (12).

c. Tack by catching a little bit of fabric at X marks with a buttonhole stitch to hold the bar in place on the arc line. As you approach the second needle, move it to a point halfway between the last stitch and the end point. Remove the second needle entirely near end of bar.

d. When working several concentric bands next to each other, work the outside one first. To lay the strands for the remaining bands, place the second needle slightly inside the previous band—about 1/16" (2 mm)—and be sure laid strands are pulled down inside the previous band (13).

e. Work buttonhole over each set of strands, tacking at three points and moving or removing second needle as needed.

f. The ridge of the second and subsequent bands should just barely overlay the inside edge of the previous band (14).

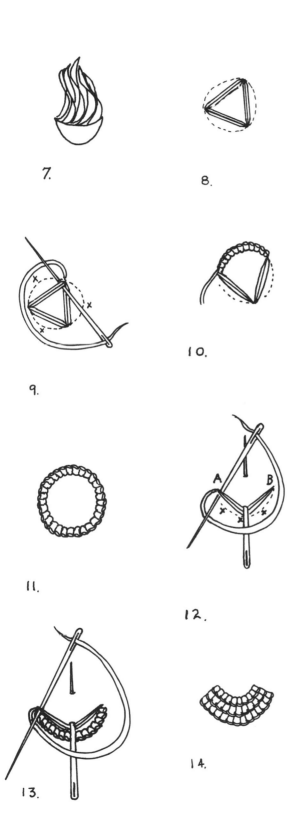

7.

8.

9.

10.

11.

12.

13.

14.

24. Double Buttonhole Stitch

This stitch makes a broad line that can be used for stems, edges of motifs, or borders. Its width depends on the length of the stitches (3-28).

a. Make a line of buttonhole stitches, spaced the width of your yarn apart (1).

b. Turn work and make a second line of buttonhole, fitting these stitches into the spaces left by the first row (2). A completed line is shown in (3). These stitches may be perpendicular to the working line or slanted at an angle (4).

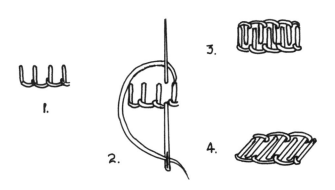

3-28. Double buttonhole stitch.

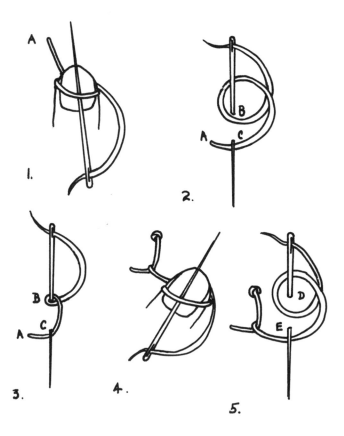

3-29. Knotted buttonhole stitch.

25. Knotted Buttonhole Stitch

This stitch results in an open buttonhole with a knot on the end of each stitch. Work from left to right (3-29).

a. Needle up at A. Hold the yarn down with the left thumb and wrap the yarn over the thumb from right to left and under the thumb again, with the yarn emerging at the right side of the thumb. Slip the needle into this loop from bottom to top (1).

b. Slide the loop off the thumb and take the needle down at B and up at C, the point of needle extending over the yarn coming from A (2).

c. Tighten the yarn around the needle (3).

d. Pull through and hold the yarn down with the thumb as in the first step.

e. Wrap the yarn around the thumb as before and place the needle in loop (4).

f. Slip the loop off the thumb, take the needle down at D, up at E (5).

g. Tighten the yarn around the needle and pull through. Continue working stitches as above, taking care to space the stitches evenly.

26. Open Buttonhole Stitch (Blanket Stitch)

The only difference in working this variation is that the stitches are spaced apart rather than placed next to each other. This spacing can be adjusted to fit the situation (3-30). In order to present a neat appearance, however, the spacing between stitches must be even (1). This stitch may be used when you do not want a solid look but rather an open, airy, or feathery appearance. Stitch lengths may be varied so that a pattern is formed; (2, 3) show two possible patterns.

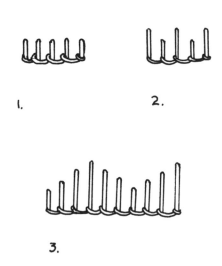

3-30. Open buttonhole stitch (blanket stitch).

27. Reverse Buttonhole Stitch

This variation of the buttonhole stitch can be used in areas where you want a spiny appearance with the spines reversed to the outside. They may be worked perpendicular to the working line or at an angle to it (3-31).

a. Needle up at A, down at B outside the area being worked, and up on the working line C (1).

b. Needle down at D, up at E for the second stitch (2); (3) shows a circle completed. The stitch can also be worked in patterns other than a circle.

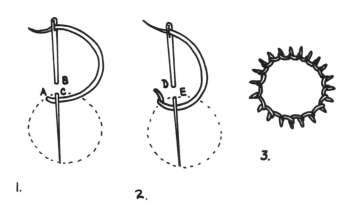

3-31. *Reverse buttonhole stitch.*

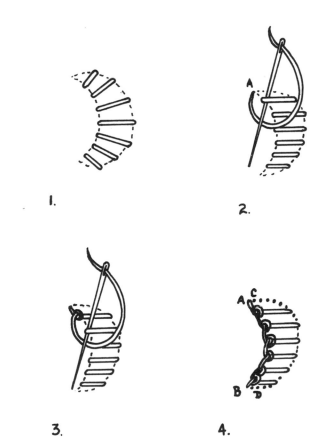

3-32. *Raised buttonhole stitch.*

28. Raised Buttonhole Stitch

The raised buttonhole stitch is worked over horizontal bars laid about ⅛" (3 mm) apart or slightly less, depending on the weight of the yarn (3-32). They may be straight across or slightly fanned (1) if the area being filled lends itself to this arrangement. If the yarn is light or fine, use double strands for laying the bars, use a tight tension on the bars, and extend them a needle's width outside the lines (or the lines may not be covered when the work is completed). No bar should lie directly on either the top or the bottom line. If the area to be filled is curved, start at the top and at the inside curve.

a. Using a single strand of yarn and a tapestry needle, needle up at A, loop the yarn down and to the right, slip the needle under the first bar, top to bottom, needle coming over the looped yarn (2).

b. Pull through and slip the needle under the second bar, looping yarn as before (3).

c. Pull through, with needle coming over the looped yarn. After pulling each stitch through, tighten between the bars by rocking the yarn gently first up and away from yourself, then back toward yourself, while keeping a firm but gentle tension on the yarn. This motion will firm up the yarn between the bars, but be careful not to pull the bars out of line.

d. Continue working down one bar at a time until the bottom is reached.

e. Needle down on bottom line B (4).

f. On the back of the work return the yarn to the top (slipping under stitches or catching fabric at a few points), since all the rows of stitching must be worked in the same direction.

g. Work the next row just to the right of the first row, coming up at C, working down one bar at a time, then down at D next to B at the bottom. Dots on (4) indicate the points for bringing the needle up and down as you work subsequent rows. These points should be directly adjacent to each other.

h. After the first row push slightly against the previous rows with the needle as you slip it under a bar. Do not crowd too many rows into the space, or the pattern made by the stitch will be obliterated. Aim to just cover the fabric. If the end bars are shorter than the others, discontinue working them when filled and work on the remaining bars.

29. Tailor's Buttonhole Stitch

This version of the buttonhole stitch resembles the close buttonhole, except that the ridge portion is more raised and obvious. It is produced by twisting the yarn before pulling it through (3-33).

a. First make a straight stitch AB as in the close buttonhole (21), with the needle coming up again at A.

b. Needle down at C, up at D. Take the yarn coming from the eye of the needle and pass it under the point of the needle from right to left (1).

c. Pull through.

d. Make another stitch to the right of the last one, pass the yarn under the point of the needle as before, and pull through.

e. Continue in same manner; (2) shows several stitches.

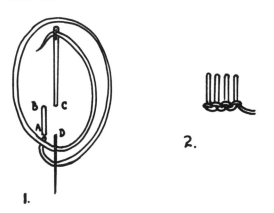

3-33. Tailor's buttonhole stitch.

30. Wallingford Stitch

This variation of the open buttonhole stitch was initiated at the Wallingford Crewel Studio in Pennsylvania. It can be worked either with a single strand of yarn for small motifs or with double or heavy yarn for large motifs. It is especially effective for the latter, making a beautiful border for a motif with an open filler (3-34).

a. Make an open buttonhole stitch (1).

b. Make a small chain stitch over the right-hand corner of the same stitch (2). Pull through (3).

c. Continue making first an open buttonhole stitch, then a small chain over the corner of that stitch. The width of the open buttonhole should be such that it can be filled with a double strand of yarn or two straight stitches when worked in double yarn or with a single strand when worked singly.

d. Fill the spaces of the open stitches with either one or two strands of a strongly contrasting value of the color used (4).

e. After filling is completed, the inside or open edge may need to be outlined in some manner.

31. Wheel Buttonhole Stitch

This is an open buttonhole stitch worked inside a circle, with the inside end of all stitches being placed in the same hole (3-35).

a. This point may be in the center of the circle (1), or it may be located off-center for a different effect (4).

b. Start as indicated (1). Continue as in (2).

c. Stitches should be spaced evenly, except, perhaps, when the shared hole is located off-center. In this case the stitches on the narrower side may be worked closer together.

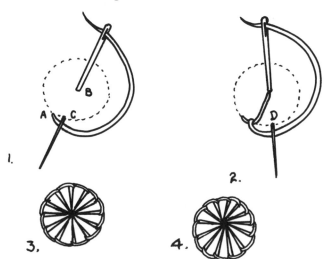

3-35. Wheel buttonhole stitch.

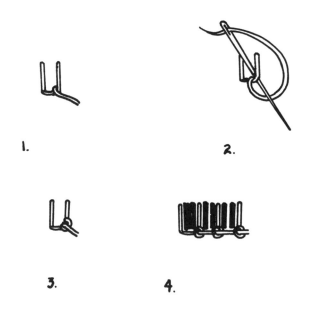

3-34. Wallingford stitch.

OTHER LOOPED STITCHES

32. Cretan Stitch

The Cretan stitch offers almost endless possibilities and variations, resulting in great differences in the finished appearance. It may be worked closed for a solid effect, open for a lighter feeling, slanted or almost horizontal, or with the center portion of the stitch close together or spread farther apart. Each of these factors produces a different finished effect. Because of these numerous possibilities this stitch is useful in disciplined embroidery as well as in a free, modern style of stitchery. Here is how to work the stitch solidly or closed (3-36).

a. Mark two guidelines, one on either side of center dotted line (1).

b. Needle up at A at the outer tip of the leaf or petal.

c. Loop the yarn down and to the right, needle down at B just barely below and to the right of A on the outside leaf line, up at C below on the right guideline (1).

d. Pull the needle through, coming over the looped yarn.

e. Loop the yarn toward the left, needle down at D, just barely to the left of and below A on the outer line; up at E on left guideline (2).

f. Pull through, with the needle coming over the looped yarn.

g. Loop the yarn to the right, down at F, up at G (3).

h. Pull through and continue working stitches on alternate sides.

i. Each stitch should fit itself around the last stitch made without fabric showing between stitches. Since the stitches are worked alternately, first one side and then the other, the work may be started either on the right or the left side. Note that the needle goes down on the right outside line, is looped to the right, and comes up on the right guideline, or just the reverse on the left. Do not pack too many stitches into the space. Guidelines may be spread more for a different finished appearance, especially on a wide leaf (5).

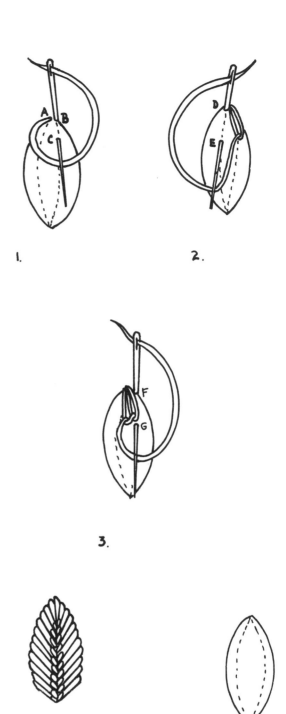

1.   2.

3.

4.   5.

3-36. Cretan stitch.

33. Feather Stitch

This stitch was often used by our mothers and grandmothers to decorate baby clothes, since it makes a fine and delicate line of stitching (3-37). Think of three equal spaces made by four vertical lines (1).

a. Needle up at A, loop the yarn to the right, needle down at B, and up at C (1).

b. Pull through, needle coming over the looped yarn.

c. Loop the yarn to the left, needle down at D, up at E (2).

d. Pull through, needle coming over looped yarn. Note that B drops below A and that C is below B. D is opposite C and E is below D, F is opposite E, and H is opposite G, and so on. The effect can be varied by changing the width of the center space and the distance the stitches drop below the previous stitches. Feather stitch can be worked inside a leaf, then outlined (4).

e. Use the vertical lines when practicing. Once you get the idea of the stitch placement, you will be able to gauge this spacing by eye.

34. Closed Fly Stitch

The fly stitch is one of the most useful leaf stitches that the embroiderer has at her disposal. It can be worked as an open stitch or as a closed stitch, as well as on very small leaves. It is wise to use the fly stitch on a leaf that has a decided curve, because it can be controlled without interrupting the pattern made by the stitch. On the fabric mark a center line on the leaf. This will serve as a guideline for the tie-down stitches (3-38).

a. Needle up at A, at the tip or the end of the leaf, down at B on the center line. The length of this stitch will establish the slant for the remaining stitches and should be longer on long, narrow leaves than on short, fat ones (1). Never make it more than one-fourth the length of the leaf or more than ¼" (6 mm).

b. Needle up at C on the outer leaf line, just below and to the left of A.

c. Loop the yarn down and to the right.

d. Needle down at D on the outer leaf line, just below and to the right of A.

e. Needle up at B again in the same hole, the needle coming over the looped yarn (2).

f. Pull through until stitch lies flat.

g. Make small tie-down stitch going down at E (3).

h. Continue working down the leaf, placing the stitches next to each other so that no fabric shows between them and moving down the outside and center lines the width of the yarn with each stitch. This will maintain the slant of the stitches. If the outer ends of stitches drop too quickly, the slant will decrease and flatten out. Try to keep the slant on the two sides about the same. If the leaf curves strongly on one side, the slant will soon be steeper on the longer, curved side than on the other side. When this occurs, bring the needle up on the outer edge of the steeper side, then tuck the point of the needle under the last tie-down stitch at center. Continue making complete stitches until another fill-in stitch is needed (5). Stitches A and B emerge from the same tie-down stitch. Continue working until the leaf is filled, being careful not to crowd in too many stitches. This stitch is prettier when each strand of yarn is clearly visible, not crowded together.

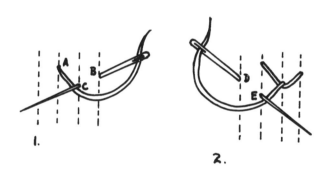

1.

2.

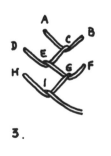

3.

4.

3-37. Feather stitch.

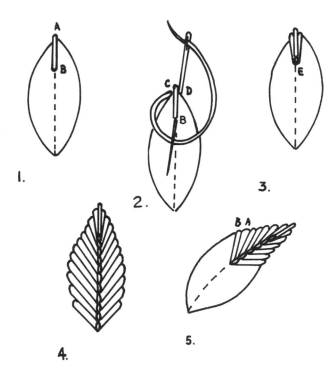

3-38. Closed fly stitch.

3-39. Serrated fly stitch.   *3-40. Open fly stitch.*

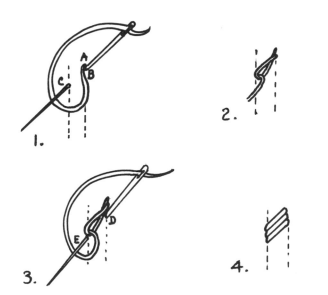

3-41. Rope stitch.

35. Serrated Fly Stitch

A variation of the fly stitch alternates the usual stitches that fall on the leaf line with slightly longer ones that extend a bit beyond it. This results in a serrated edge on the leaf (3-39).

36. Open Fly Stitch

To work an open fly stitch, space the stitches an even distance apart. The size of the leaf will influence this spacing, since it should be proportioned to the leaf size. The length of the tie-down stitches must equal the space between stitches on the outside edge of leaf, which will then need to be outlined in some manner (3-40).

37. Rope Stitch

The rope stitch resembles a slanted satin stitch worked between two parallel lines, but the left side has a wrapped or raised appearance. The stitch can be worked with the wrapped side on the right, but this is a bit awkward for a right-handed person. It can be done with a sewing stitch, but the smoothness of the stitch depends on accurate placement, which is best achieved with stab stitching (3-41).

   a. Needle up at A on right line, down at B just below A. Loop yarn and bring needle up at C (1).

   b. Pull through. Result is an elongated, slanted, twisted chain (2).

   c. Needle down at D just below B. Keep holding the yarn toward the right (holding it down with the left thumb) as it comes from the first stitch so you can clearly see the left line. Bring needle up at E just below C (3).

   d. Continue working stitches as above, being careful to place stitches exactly on lines and maintaining a 45-degree angle (4).

   e. Keep the stitches on right line tucked in under previous stitches and use an even tension on all stitches. If possible, keep the wrapped side of the work on the outside of the curve if the working lines are not straight.

   f. The width of the stitch can be narrowed by gradually dropping the points at which the needle comes up on the left line and by narrowing the space between the lines until you are working on a single line.

38. Scroll Stitch

This stitch is most effective when worked with a firm thread, though it can be worked with either a single finer yarn and close stitches or with double yarn. It makes a beautiful edging. It can be worked from left to right, as is shown in most books, but a right-handed person will find it more comfortable and natural to work from right to left (3-42).

a. Needle up at A on the working line, loop the yarn up to the left, then down and to the right.

b. Make a small, vertical stitch BC from top to bottom under working line and within the loop formed by the yarn (1).

c. Holding the thumb over the yarn just to the left of B, pull through until only a small loop remains. Then pull straight up until the stitch is formed (2).

d. Loop the yarn as in the first step, take stitch DE coming over looped yarn (3).

e. Pull through as for the first stitch; (4) shows three completed stitches. The stitches must be even in size, evenly spaced, and pulled with the same tension. Check the back of the work for regularity of stitch size and spacing and experiment with different spacings to determine the best for the thread you are using.

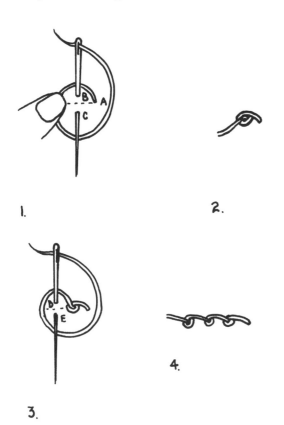

1.

2.

3.

4.

3-42. Scroll stitch.

FLAT STITCHES

This is the largest of all the stitch groups. Flat stitches are for the most part fairly simple stitches made up of various combinations of individual stitches placed in straight, angled, or crossed positions. Flat stitches can be worked on straight or curved lines, side by side to fill spaces, or detached and scattered as fillers.

Color Key
G 1, 2—green wool
BF 1, 2—blue floss
YF 1, 2—yellow floss
WF—white floss
GF—green floss
YP 1, 2—yellow Perle
BP 1, 2—blue Perle
WP—white Perle
The lowest number indicates the lightest value.

Stitch Key
40 whipped back stitch
41 laced back stitch
42 Pekinese stitch
46 double cross-stitch
48 fern stitch
49 fishbone stitch
50 open fishbone stitch
51 serrated fishbone stitch
52 shaded fishbone stitch
63 outline
65 whipped outline stitch
66 alternating stem stitch
67 Portuguese stem stitch
68 raised stem stitch
73 satin stitch
74 slanted satin stitch
75 Guilloche stitch
78 straight stitch
84 French knot

1. Work the ribs of the fan in whipped outline stitch using two strands of floss for the outline stitch and one for whipping.

2. Work the flowers with two strands of floss.

3. Work the fern stitch with one strand of floss.

4. Work the laced back stitch and the Guilloche stitch after the adjacent parts are completed. Then work the ring on the fan and the ribbon.

3-43. Sampler #1 illustrating many of the flat
stitches, worked on brown British satin in Appleton
yarn, D.M.C. embroidery floss, and D.M.C. Perle
cotton #8.

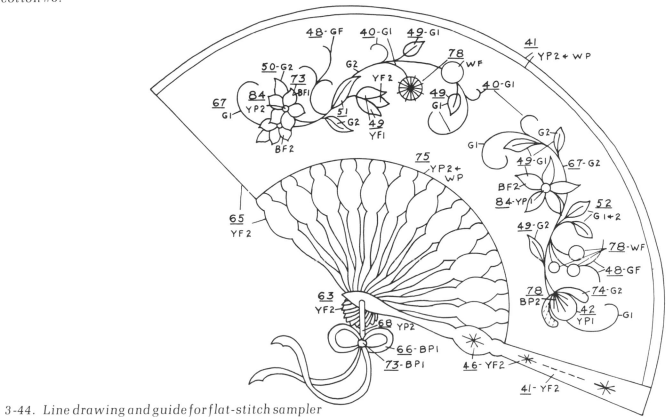

3-44. Line drawing and guide for flat-stitch sampler
#1.

3-45. Sampler #2 illustrating more flat stitches,
worked on blue Aida cloth in Appleton yarn and
D.M.C. embroidery floss and Perle cotton #8.

3-46. Line drawing and guide for flat-stitch sampler #2.

Color Key
R 1, 2, 3—rose wool
RP—rose Perle cotton
G 1, 2, 3—green wool
GP—green Perle cotton
BP—blue Perle cotton
BF 1, GF 1—blue and gray floss
WP—white Perle cotton
B 1—black wool
BR—brown wool
Gr 1, 2, 3—gray wool
W—white wool
The lowest number indicates the lightest value.

Stitch Key
46 double cross-stitch
47 cross-stitch flowers
49 fishbone stitch
63 outline stitch
65 whipped outline stitch
73 satin stitch
76 twisted satin stitch
77 split stitch
78 straight stitch
79 Algerian-eye border stitch
80 Turkeywork stitch

1. Raccoon—work the eyes, nose, and tongue (or mouth) in satin stitch. Outline the eyes with white split stitch. Work the ears, hands, and feet in split stitch, the latter two in black and the former in gray. Outline the ears with black outline stitch. Do the turkeywork following the picture for placement of values and using darker values to separate arms and legs from the rest of the body. Use a color about two values lighter than you want the finished result to be, since cut turkeywork always appears darker than the wool itself seems to be. Use white, very light grays, medium grays, and black. You may follow the picture in this book or find one of your own to use as a guide when working the raccoon. Trim carefully. You may sculpture the trimming to simulate the shape of the body and to round the arms, legs, and tail.

2. Mouse—work the eyes in black satin stitch, with a little white around the eyes. Work nose and inside the ears in rose or pink satin stitch, then outline ears with brown outline stitch. Work body and face in split stitch, following the picture for placement of colors and values. The tail is worked in whipped outline after the leaf underneath it is completed.

3. Mushroom—work the cap, stem, and underpart in split stitch using white, grays, and rose, following picture for their placement. The outer edge of the cap is outlined in white split stitch.

4. The leaves on top of the mushroom stem can be worked over split-stitch edges to raise them up. Use about three values of greens. Mix green and brown straight stitches for the ground.

5. Flower—work in solid outline stitch, making rows close together, using partial rows where necessary, and placing values as shown in the picture to give the needed shading. Stop one value and bring up the next one as if you were continuing with the first value. These threads need not be finished off but can be brought to the top of the work out of your way. They can then be pulled to the back when needed again. Work stem of flower over raccoon's body.

6. Raindrops—use very light blue or gray floss worked in a satin stitch.

7. Border—use blue, green, and white Perle, #8, for Algerian-eye-stitch border, following picture for placement of colors.

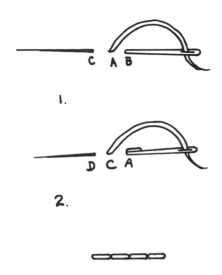

1.

2.

3.

3-47. Back stitch.

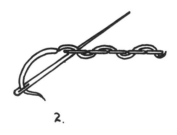

1.

2.

3.

3-48. Whipped back stitch.

39. Back Stitch

The back stitch follows curves especially well, is equally useful on straight lines, and has numerous lovely variations. Its success depends upon even spacing of the individual stitches. It is a good choice for the small initials used for signing an embroidery (3-47).

a. Needle up at A, down at B, and up at C(1). Pull through.

b. Needle down again at A in the same hole, up at D (2). Pull through; (3) shows four consecutive stitches. The size of the stitches will be governed by the weight of the thread used as well as by the line stitched, such as a sharp or gradual curve.

40. Whipped Back Stitch

When whipped the back stitch has a raised, corded effect (3-48). Always slip the needle under the stitches from the same side, picking up no fabric (1). The dotted lines indicate the needle positions for subsequent stitches. Pull (after every third or fourth stitch) until the line of whipping is smooth (2).

41. Threaded or Laced Back Stitch

The lacing thread may be the same as that used for the back stitch, in a contrasting color or texture, or both (3-49). It is passed under the back stitches, without going into the fabric, from alternating sides (1). It may be threaded in only one direction or threaded in the reverse direction (2, 3). The lacing thread should be left slightly relaxed.

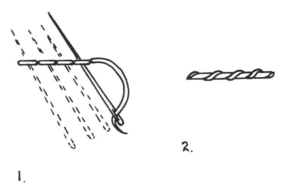

1.

2.

3-49. Threaded back stitch.

42. Pekinese Stitch

This is a particularly lovely version of the back stitch. It was known as the forbidden stitch in China because it was worked with such tiny stitches and in such poor light that the workers became blind. Entire embroideries were worked in this stitch alone. It can be used as a line stitch or to fill an area (3-50).

a. Work a line of back stitch with each stitch about ⅛" (3mm) long—smaller for a fine yarn, a bit longer for heavier. The interlacing thread may be the same as that used for the back stitch or contrast in both color and texture.

b. Needle up at A, left end of the row of back stitch. Using a tapestry needle, slip under the second stitch from the end, bottom to top, not going into fabric (1).

c. Pull the thread most of the way through, leaving a small loop underneath. Slip the needle, top to bottom, under first stitch from the left end and over the loop coming from A (2).

d. Pull through, adjusting the tension of the lacing thread on both the bottom and the top and leaving it slightly relaxed.

e. Slip the needle, bottom to top, under the third back stitch (3). Pull almost through.

f. Slip the needle, top to bottom, under the second back stitch and over the loop on the bottom (4).

g. Pull through and adjust tension on bottom and top of lacing thread.

h. Continue, moving ahead one stitch as needle goes up and coming down into the previous stitch.

i. End by taking the needle down at the end of the row at B (4). The lacing thread should lie close to the back stitches and should be relaxed but not too loopy. The bottom will be flatter than the top of the finished interlaced line. This fact can be used to advantage when working the stitch into a design, depending on whether you want a flat or a scalloped edge to the motif. Make all loops of the lacing thread the same size. Hold the left thumb over the last completed stitches when pulling the next stitch through to prevent changing the tension on the previous stitches.

43. Laced Cretan Stitch

This stitch could be included with the regular Cretan stitch, but, since it is based on the back stitch, it has been placed here (3-51).

a. Work two rows of back stitch, placing the ends of the stitches of one row directly opposite the center of the stitches of the other row.

b. Using the same or a contrasting thread, bring the needle up at A (1).

c. Loop the yarn down and to the right, slip the needle, no fabric, under the first back stitch on right line of back stitch, the needle coming over the looped yarn (1).

d. Pull through, loop the yarn down and to the left, slip the needle under the first back stitch on the left line of back stitch and over the looped yarn (2).

e. Pull through, loop the yarn down and to the right, slip the needle under the second stitch on right line and over the looped yarn (3).

f. Pull through and continue alternating sides. The tension should be such that the back stitches are not pulled out of line.

g. End by taking the needle down at B (3) between the two lines of back stitch. The two lines of back stitch may be parallel or may curve and taper at one or both ends.

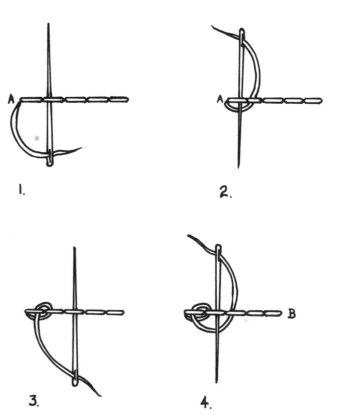

1.

2.

3.

4.

3-50. Pekinese stitch.

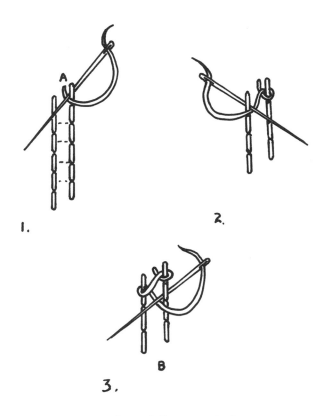

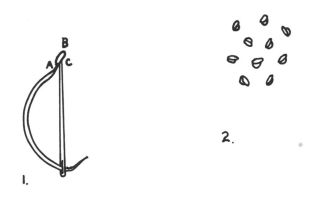

3-51. Laced Cretan stitch.

3-52. Seed stitch.

44. Seed Stitch

This stitch gives a light, open filling. It can be worked in one value alone or in several values to give the effect of shading. The spacing can produce the same effect, appearing darker when the stitches are placed close together and lighter when they are spaced further apart. A combination of both can be used for even greater effectiveness (3-52).

a. Needle up at A, down at B, making a small, straight stitch.

b. Needle up at A again, down at C about two-thirds the distance from A to B, with point of needle tucked in under stitch AB (1). This second small stitch gives added dimension to the stitch. Do not pull either stitch too tight—it should be slightly puffy.

c. Work the stitches in random directions (2).

45. Cross-stitch

Every little girl who has embroidered is familiar with the cross-stitch. It is easiest to work this stitch on an even-weave fabric in which the threads can be counted. When using other fabrics, stitching may be simplified by using a cross-stitch canvas, which can be basted onto the ground fabric and worked over without stitching into the canvas threads. These can then be carefully removed when the embroidery is completed. Cross-stitch has been widely used for several hundred years in Europe, as well as in this country, where its most common use was for samplers. Cross-stitch should be worked in straight lines in order to get an even crossing, and all individual stitches must be crossed in the same direction (3-53).

a. Work all lines that go in the same direction first (1). In some instances it is more convenient to complete each stitch before going on to the next one.

b. Working back across this row of stitches, put in the remaining parts of the crosses in the opposite direction (2).

c. The individual crosses may be separated, touching, or arranged in a pattern to form a border (3).

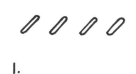

3-53. Cross-stitch.

46. Double Cross-stitch

This variation (3-54) is simply a straight cross-stitch superimposed on a diagonal one (1) or vice versa (2). Patterns can be created with this version as well as with the regular cross-stitch.

3-54. Double cross-stitch.

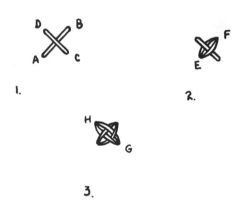

3-55. Cross-stitch flowers.

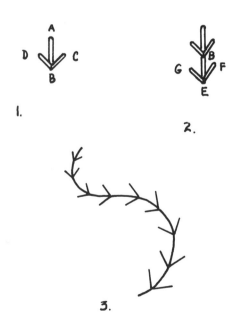

3-56. Fern stitch.

47. Cross-stitch Flowers

This version can be used in the same situations as can the regular cross-stitch, or it can be used to make small flowers. It is a bit more ornate and has more dimension (3-55).

a. Work a conventional cross-stitch, AB and CD (1).

b. Using the same holes, make the first half of another cross-stitch, EF (2). Do not pull it too tight.

c. Needle up at C to start the second half of the second cross, GH. Go over strand EF of the second cross and under strand AB of the first cross (3). Use the back of the needle to prevent splitting the first thread.

48. Fern Stitch

The fern stitch is a composite of straight stitches and is useful for making fine, lacy greenery in situations that need a light touch rather than the heavier appearance of leaves. It curves nicely in any direction (3-56).

a. Make three straight stitches AB, CB, and DB, with line AB slightly longer than the other two (1).

b. Make another group of three stitches EB, FE, and GE (2).

c. Continue working in groups of threes, following the stem line. At the tip end of the frond the stitches can be made fairly small, gradually increasing in size toward the base end (3).

49. Fishbone Stitch

This stitch is an old standby for working leaves but can be just as useful for making flower petals. It is worked by making a series of straight, slanted stitches that cross each other in the center of the leaf. A satisfactory finished appearance depends upon whether these crossovers, which indicate the center vein of the leaf, form a neat line. For this reason it is usually wise to use this stitch on a fairly straight leaf, leaving the fly stitch (34) for decidedly curved leaves, which require some fill-in stitches on the longer side. It is more difficult to put in these extra stitches without breaking the pattern with the fishbone stitch than with the fly stitch.

a. Mark a guideline down the center of the leaf (3-57).

b. Needle up at A at the tip end of the leaf and down at B on the center line (1). The length of this stitch will establish the slant for all the following stitches. It should be at least 3/16″ (5 mm) but never more than one-quarter the length of the leaf.

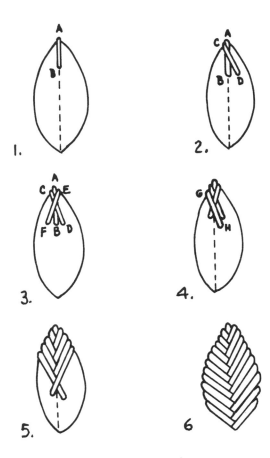

3-57. *Fishbone stitch.*

3-58. *Open fishbone stitch.*

3-59. *Serrated fishbone stitch.*

c. Needle up at C on the outside line and just to the left of A, down at D, crossing the yarn over the first stitch and on the same level as B (2).

d. Needle up at E just to the right of A and down at F, even with B and D and crossing over the first two stitches (3).

e. The next stitch GH crosses over stitch EF (4).

f. Continue working down the leaf (5), alternating sides and placing each stitch just below the previous one so that no fabric shows between them but being careful not to pack the stitches too close to each other.

g. The last pair of stitches should meet at the center bottom of the leaf (6).

h. The inside end of a stitch must drop somewhat below the last stitch in order to maintain the same slant. Lay the working yarn just below the previous stitch and in the same direction in order to determine where to place the inside end of that stitch. If the leaf is slightly curved, the inside ends of the stitches on the longer, more curved side must be kept a bit closer to the ends of stitches directly above them than to the ends of the stitches on the other side of the leaf. This keeps the crossover line straighter and in the center of the leaf. The ends of the stitches on the outside of the leaf must be placed only the width of the yarn apart. Making this space wider not only results in poor coverage of fabric but loses the slant so that the stitches gradually flatten out.

50. Open Fishbone Stitch
In this variation of the fishbone stitch some of the fabric is left showing between the stitches (3-58). All the spaces must be kept the same for a neat appearance. Place the inside ends of the stitches so that they will be covered by the following stitch and will not extend beyond it. The leaf must be outlined in some manner in order to cover the line of the leaf.

51. Serrated Fishbone Stitch
The edges of a leaf worked in fishbone stitch can be serrated by placing the ends of alternate stitches slightly beyond the outside line (3-59).

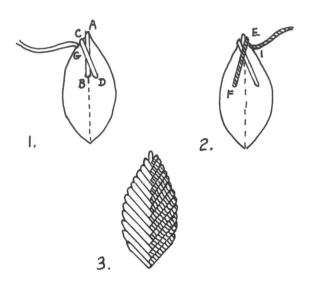

3-60. Shaded fishbone stitch.

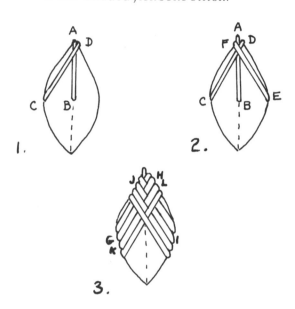

3-61. Raised fishbone stitch.

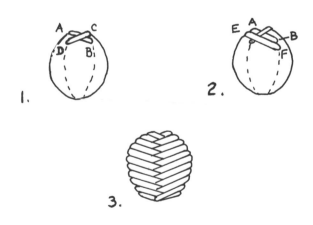

3-62. Flat stitch.

52. Shaded Fishbone Stitch

The two sides of a leaf can be worked with different values of the chosen color to produce some degree of shading. Use two needles, one for each value (3-60).

a. Make stitches AB and CD with the first needle and the first value. Bring the same needle up at G for the beginning of the next stitch on that side (1). Put that needle and yarn aside on top of the work.

b. Bring the second needle up on the other side of the leaf and make stitch EF. Bring the same needle up at I for the beginning of the next stitch on that side (2). Put that needle and yarn aside on top of the work.

c. Bringing the yarn up to start the next stitch on the same side always keeps the other needle and thread on top of the work while not in use so that it will not become tangled underneath.

d. Continue, alternating the sides and always using the same value of yarn on the same side of the leaf (3). The contrast between the two values should be apparent but not stark.

53. Raised Fishbone Stitch

The finished appearance of this version is the same as for the regular fishbone stitch, except that it has a raised, padded appearance, but the technique is different (3-61).

a. Make the first stitch AB about one-third the length of the leaf. Needle up at C on the outside line and even with B. Cross over AB (1), needle down at D.

b. Needle up at E on the opposite side of the leaf and even with B and C, down at F, crossing over AB and CD (2).

c. Continue with stitches GH, IJ, KL, and so on (3), placing the stitches so that each lies directly under the previous one. The needle will always come up on one outside line and go down on the opposite line. The last pair of stitches should meet at the bottom of the leaf. The finished pattern will look like the regular fishbone stitch (49).

54. Flat Stitch

The flat stitch closely resembles the fishbone stitch, except that it is flatter and less angled and there is no beginning vertical stitch (3-62).

a. Needle up at A and down at B, then up at C on the opposite side and down at D (1).

b. Needle up at E, just below A, and down at F just below B (2).

c. Continue, alternating sides until the space is filled (3).

55. Open Herringbone Stitch

The herringbone stitch has numerous variations. It can be worked between parallel lines or in a space that tapers at one or both ends. It was often used in early American embroideries, but its history reaches as far back as the early 14th century, where it appears as a decoration on clothing in paintings. All the herringbone stitches require even spacing. This is easier to accomplish if even-weave fabric is used so that threads can be counted. On other fabrics the spacing must be judged by eye, so it is a good idea to practice this stitch before putting it into a design (3-63).

a. Needle up at A on the left end, bottom line (it can be started on either line), and down at B diagonally to the right (1).

b. Needle up at C, a short distance to the left of B on the top line, then down at D on the lower line diagonally to the right (2). Space BC on the top should be centered between AD on the bottom.

c. Needle up at E directly below B and down at F on the top line. Space AE should be equal to BF: (3) shows this stitch and those that follow.

d. The appearance of the stitch can be changed by making the spacing between the stitches either smaller or larger, but all diagonal lines going in one direction must be parallel. The only exception is stitching done between curved lines. This is tricky, since the spacing on the inside or shorter curve must be less than that on the outer, longer curve.

56. Closed Herringbone Stitch

The only difference between this version and the open herringbone stitch is that the ends of the individual crosses touch instead of being separated (3-64).

a. Needle up at A, down at B (1).

b. Needle up at C, down at D (2). The distance BC is half the distance AD and is centered between A and D. Once the spacing of these two stitches is properly established, the subsequent stitches are easily spaced, following the same pattern.

c. Needle up at E midway between A and D, then down at F (3), up at B, down at G (4). Distances between A and E, E and D, B and C, and B and F are equal.

d. Start the next stitch with the needle up at E. Once this much of the pattern is established, it is easy to continue in the same manner; (5) shows the finished pattern.

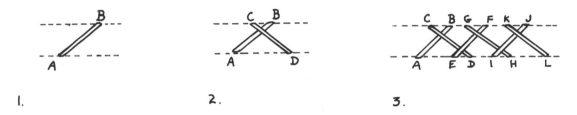

3-63. Open herringbone stitch.

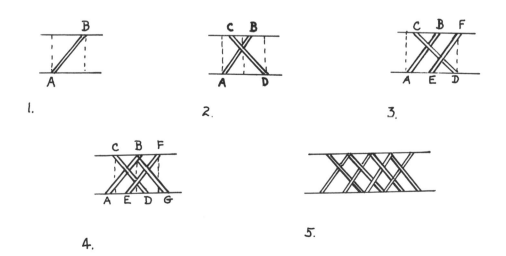

3-64. Closed herringbone stitch.

1.

2.

3-65. Tied herringbone stitch.

3-66. Threaded or laced herringbone stitch.

57. Tied Herringbone Stitch

Either the open or the closed herringbone stitch may be tied down with the same or a contrasting yarn (3-65). This must be done if the stitches are long or if they might catch and be pulled loose (1). It can also be tied down with the coral knot stitch (2).

58. Threaded or Laced Herringbone Stitch

Both the open and the closed herringbone stitches may also be laced or threaded, again with yarn that contrasts in color, texture, or both. The interlacing thread goes under the diagonal strands and over the crossed intersections at both top and bottom (3-66).

59. Double Herringbone Stitch

Here is how to make a double herringbone stitch (3-67).

a. Make an open herringbone but slip all the stitches under the strand of the previous stitch, moving up rather than over it (1). CD goes under AB, GH goes under EF, and so on.

b. Using a contrasting thread, work a second row of open herringbone as indicated by the dark thread, fitting this row into the spaces of the first row (2) and following these directions: stitch 1-2 slips under CD, stitch 3-4 slips under 1-2 and over EF, stitch 5-6 goes over 3-4 and under GH, stitch 7-8 slips under 5-6 and over IJ, and so on. All stitches moving down diagonally from left to right will go under, over, under. All stitches moving up diagonally from left to right will go over, under, over.

1.

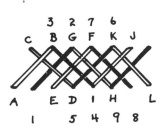

2.

3-67. Double herringbone stitch.

60. Crisscross Herringbone Stitch

If the herringbone stitch needs to cover a fairly wide area, the crisscross version is a good choice, since it covers space quickly. Work as for closed herringbone, spacing stitches as indicated below (3-68).

a. Points A, B, C, and D make a square.

b. Point E is one-third the distance between A and D, and BF is the same size as space AE.

c. Point G is one-third the distance between B and C, and space DH is the same as CG.

d. Point I is midway between E and D, and point K is midway between B and G.

e. From this point follow the established pattern.

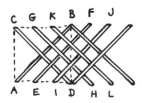

3-68. Crisscross herringbone stitch.

61. Close Herringbone Stitch

This version of the herringbone stitch covers the fabric completely. It can be worked between two lines or used to work a leaf. The finished appearance is almost identical to the raised fishbone stitch, producing a padded, raised effect that makes it useful in situations in which a leaf needs depth in order to raise it above the surrounding embroidery (3-69).

a. Needle up at A, about one-third the length of the leaf from tip, down at B at the tip of leaf, up at C directly across from A, and down at B again (1).

b. Needle up at D below A and down at E just below B, crossing over stitch BC (2).

c. Needle up at F just below C and down at G, crossing over both previous stitches (3).

d. Continue, alternating sides and placing each new strand so that it lies directly below the last strand going in the same direction (4).

e. (5) shows the completed leaf, and (6) shows the stitch being worked between two lines.

f. Keep a good slant on the stitches by dropping down a bit at D, F, and subsequent points where the needle comes up. This is necessary as long as the shape of the leaf is widening; as it narrows, the points at which the needle comes up will not need to drop as much in order to maintain the same slant.

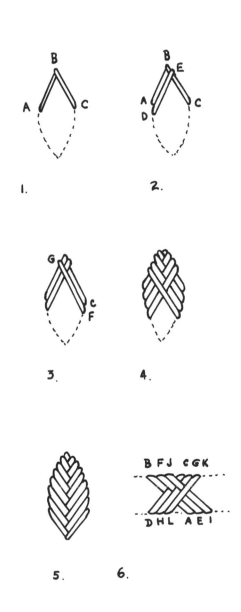

3-69. Close herringbone stitch.

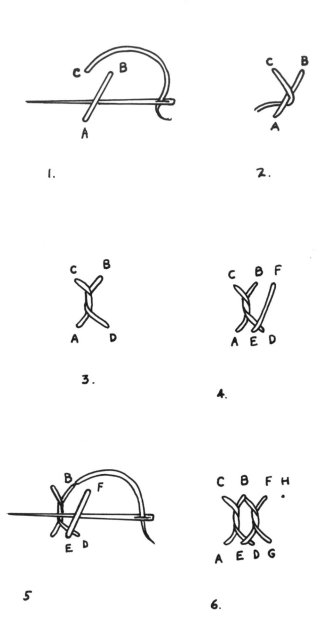

1.

2.

3.

4.

5

6.

3-70. Breton stitch.

62. Breton Stitch

This stitch is basically worked like the closed herringbone stitch, but the spacing is different and the upward-slanted stitch is wrapped (3-70).

a. Needle up at A, down at B, up at C above A (1). Do not pull this stitch too tight.

b. Slip the needle from right to left under AB, no fabric (1)

c. Pull through (2), needle down at D below and slightly to the right of B (3).

d. Needle up at E to the left of D and down at F to the right of B (4). Spaces BC, DE, and BF are equal.

e. Slip the needle from right to left under stitch EF (5), then take the needle down at G (6). DG is equal to ED.

f. Start the next stitch by bringing the needle up at D, down at H.

g. Continue, following this established pattern. Adjust the vertical and horizontal spacing as needed according to the weight of the thread being used.

When filling an area solidly with rows of outline or stem stitch, work the outside lines first. Then fill the space between by working toward the center from both sides, using partial lines as needed to conform to the wide and narrow portions of the area. Place the rows of stitching close together so that no fabric shows between them. See the chain stitch (1) for the use of partial lines. In order to achieve shading with rows of outline or stem stitch positioned directly next to each other, use very close shades or values of yarn. Values that are too far apart will result in a banded effect.

Since outline and stem stitch yield different textures, the same stitch should be continued throughout the motif, even if one side of the motif must be worked in one direction and the other in the opposite direction in order to hold the yarn on the outside of a curve. The rows of stitching should follow the outside contour of the motif as nearly as possible. The shaping can then be gradually changed and straightened as the rows approach the center.

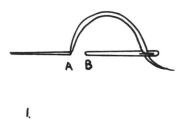

1.

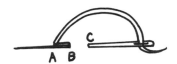

2.

3.

3-71. Outline stitch.

63. Outline Stitch

These familiar stitches are used both as line stitches and as fillers to solidly cover an area. In this latter case shading can be simulated by changing the values of the yarn color being used.

The only difference between outline and stem or crewel stitch lies in the way in which the yarn is held. For the outline stitch the yarn is held above the line when working, resulting in a fine line of stitching. For the stem stitch the yarn is held below the working line, producing a heavier, more textured line. When used on a curved line, the yarn must be held to the outside of the curve to prevent the line of stitching from "falling in." The stitch is worked from left to right. Here is how to work the basic outline stitch (3-71).

a. Needle up at A, holding the yarn up and to the right. Needle down at B and up again at A (1). The distance AB should not be more than 1/8″ (3 mm) unless very heavy yarn is used.

b. Pull through, hold the yarn up and to the right, needle down at C and up at B again in the same hole (2).

c. Pull through and continue, keeping the length of the stitches and the tension even (3). All points at which the needle goes into the fabric are on the working line.

64. Stem or Crewel Stitch

Here is how to work the stem or crewel stitch (3-72).

a. Work the same as for outline but hold the yarn below the line (1, 2, 3).

b. When working a very tight curve, hold the yarn to the outside of the curve and shorten the stitches to fit.

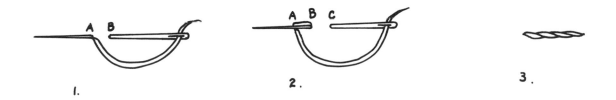

3-72. Stem stitch.

65. Whipped Outline and Stem Stitch

A smooth, raised, corded line results from whipping the outline stitch. The only other stitch that somewhat resembles this texture is the whipped back stitch, which is a bit finer. On the other hand, a whipped chain stitch gives a heavier and rougher texture. This smooth, corded appearance can be achieved only if the whipping is done from the opposite side from which the thread was held when stitching (3-73).

a. (1) shows outline stitch being whipped; the curved dotted line indicates where the yarn was held while the stitch was being worked. The needle is slipped under two strands, the first half of one stitch and the second half of another. When the needle is held at an angle as illustrated, it will naturally find its place under the two strands. No fabric is picked up by the needle. The dotted-line needles show the position of the needle for the next two whipping stitches.

b. After about three stitches pull gently but firmly on the yarn until the line of whipping is smooth; (2) shows completed whipping; (3) illustrates the procedure for whipping stem stitch.

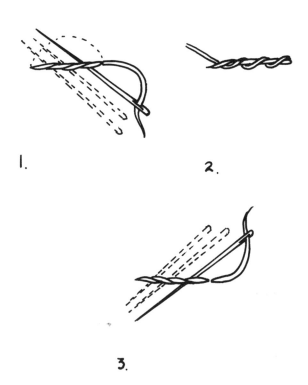

I.

2.

3.

3-73. *Whipped outline and stem stitch.*

66. Alternating Stem Stitch

For this variation the yarn is held above the working line on the first stitch, then below it for the next stitch. An interesting texture results, with one line of stitching giving the appearance of two (3-74).

a. Needle up at A, down at B, up again at A, yarn held up (1).

b. Needle down at C, up at B, yarn down (2).

c. Needle down at D, up at C, yarn up (3). Pull through.

d. Continue, alternately holding the yarn up, then down. If more than one adjacent row is to be worked, begin all rows at the left and work to the right.

e. Needle up at E, down at F, up at E again, yarn down, pull through (4).

f. Needle down at G, up at F, yarn up (5), pull through.

g. Needle down at H, up at G, yarn down (6); (7) shows two rows completed.

67. Portuguese Stem Stitch

The Portuguese stem stitch has a knotty texture and is especially beautiful when worked in a firm-textured thread such as Perle cotton; it curves well but can be used for straight lines as well (3-75).

a. Starting at the bottom, make a vertical stem stitch, needle up at A, down at B, up at C, yarn to the right (1), pull through.

b. Holding yarn up and to the left, slip the needle from right to left under stitch AB (2), pull through.

c. Yarn up and to the left again, pass needle under the same stitch a second time (3), and pull through, placing the second coil below the first coil. Pull tight.

d. Yarn down and to the right, needle down at D, up at B, pull through.

e. Yarn up and to the left, slip the needle under stitch DC, one strand only (5), pull through.

f. Yarn up and to the left, slip the needle under two strands, the bottom of the new stitch and the top of the previous stitch (6), pull tight, guiding the second coil below the first (7).

g. Note that, when the stem stitch is made, the yarn is down and to the right. When the coils are made, the yarn is up and to the left. Spacing should be such that the pairs of coils are separated from each other.

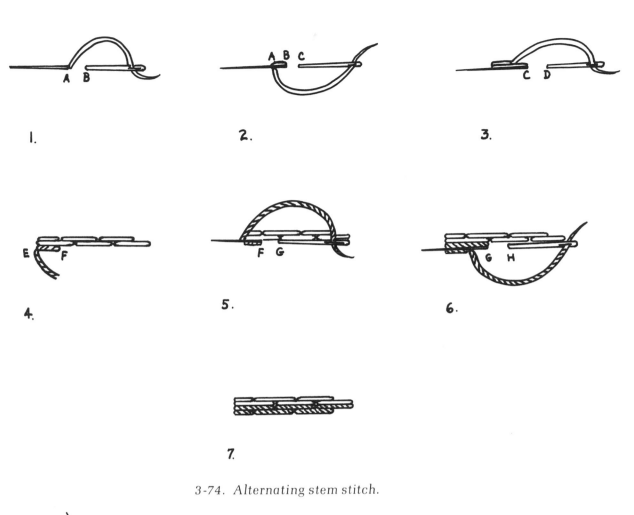

3-74. Alternating stem stitch.

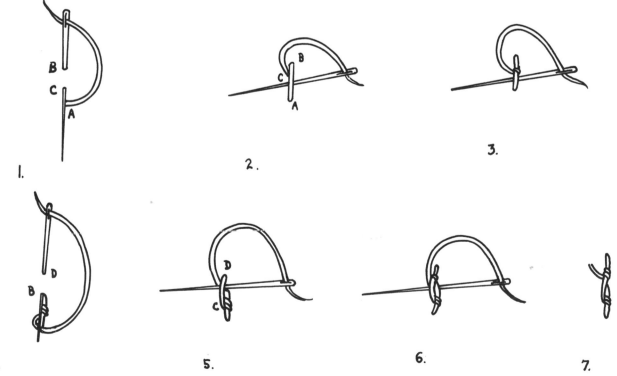

3-75. Portuguese stem stitch.

68. Raised Stem Stitch

This variation consists of stem stitch worked over bars or over padding stitches and bars. It is useful for any area that calls for a raised, textured appearance (3-76).

    a. Lay bars across the space, not more than 1/8″ (3 mm) apart, unless a heavy thread is being used.

    b. Needle up at A, left end, holding the yarn down, slip needle under the first bar, right to left, no fabric (1).

    c. Yarn down, slip the needle under the next bar (2), pull through (3).

    d. Continue, moving ahead one bar at a time and pulling only enough so that the stitch is smooth and the bars are not pulled out of line. Needle down at B, right end of the stitching (4).

    e. Return the yarn to the left end, slipping under stitches on the back to start the next row. If the distance between the ends is too great, tie off and start again at the left end.

    f. Put in only enough rows to cover the bars and the fabric. Crowding covers up the pattern made by the stitch.

69. Running Stitch

This is undoubtedly the simplest of all the stitches. It consists of a series of stitches of equal length, with all the spaces between them also equal though not necessarily the same length as that of the stitches. Several lengths and spacings of stitches are shown (3-77). There are a number of variations, which result in interesting patterns.

70. Whipped Running Stitch

The running stitch may be whipped with the same thread or with one of a contrasting color or texture (3-78).

    a. The needle is always slipped under the stitches being whipped from the same side (1).

    b. No fabric is picked up, and the yarn is carried over the line of stitching; (2) shows the result of whipping.

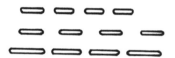

3-77. Running stitch.

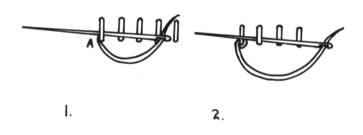

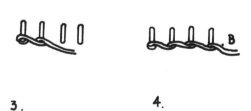

3-76. Raised stem stitch.

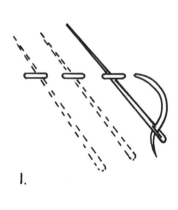

3-78. Whipped running stitch.

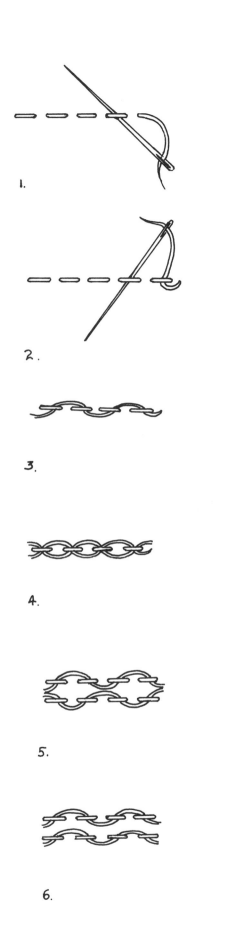

71. Threaded or Laced Running Stitch

This variation can be threaded or laced with the same thread or with one of a contrasting color or texture (3-79).

   a. The needle is passed under the first stitch from one side, no fabric (1), from the opposite side for the next stitch (2). Leave the lacing thread slightly relaxed; (3) shows several laced stitches, and (4) illustrates the lacing worked in both directions.

   b. Various patterns will result from working two or more rows of threaded running stitch close together; (5, 6) show two possible arrangements.

72. Pattern Darning Stitch

Pattern darning is the result of varying combinations of different lengths of stitches and of spaces between them (3-80). There are so many different possibilities that it is practically a subject in itself. An even-weave fabric assures evenness and regularity, which are essential for a neat result.

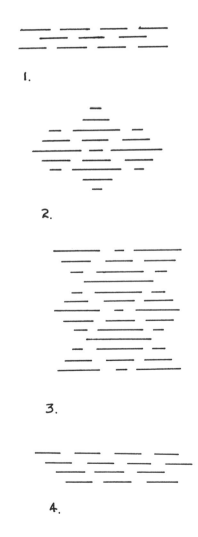

3-79. Threaded or laced running stitch.

3-80. Pattern darning stitch.

73. Satin Stitch

This stitch consists of a series of straight stitches placed side by side. Groups of satin stitches, regularly arranged, may be used as a filling. They may also be used to make a solid filling with stitches running vertically, horizontally, or diagonally. When the space to be filled is large, satin stitch is not a good choice unless the space can be broken down into several smaller areas (3-81).

a. Work a row of split, outline, or chain stitch around the outside edge. This will be completely covered and will not show when the satin stitch is completed. Its purpose is to help give a neat, even edge (1).

b. If the satin stitch is to be padded for a raised effect, use straight laidwork (88) stitches with the yarn on top of the fabric and very short stitches on the back in the opposite direction to that of the finishing stitches (2). When two layers of padding are used, make all layers run in opposing directions.

c. Needle up at A just outside the split stitch, center of the area, and down at B, also just outside the split stitch (3).

d. Working from the center to one side, place the stitches so that they lie directly next to each other, bringing the needle up on the bottom and taking it down at the top (this direction can be reversed). The needle should be in a vertical position when coming up and going down. The yarn is carried across the back (3).

e. When one side is filled, work from the center to the other side (4).

74. Slanted Satin Stitch

Here is how to work slanted satin stitch (3-82).

a. Work a row of split stitch around the outside edge in the same color as for the stitching.

b. Work the first stitch in the middle of one side (1), laying yarn in several positions to find the desired slant and bringing needle up at A, then down at B just outside split stitch.

c. Work either the stitches above or those below the first stitch, keeping them parallel and directly next to each other and making the ends of stitches even (1). Then work the other side of the center stitch.

Lay the yarn beside the last stitch to find the point at which the needle should come up and go down. This point often drops below the last stitch in order to maintain the proper slant. Work the opposite side of the leaf, following the same procedure and keeping the stitches at the same slant as on the first side of the leaf. Where the stitches meet at the center they can share the same holes as those from the other side (2).

75. Guilloche Stitch

Make evenly spaced sets of three satin stitches side by side. Using a thread of contrasting color, texture, or both and a tapestry needle, lace first in one direction. Leave the thread slightly relaxed. Then lace back in the opposite direction (3-83).

76. Twisted Satin Stitch

These stitches can be used as a scattered filler, side by side, or as small flower petals or leaves (3-84).

a. Needle up at A, down at B, and back up again at A (1).

b. Slip the needle under stitch AB, no fabric (2).

c. Needle down just barely above B (3). Do not pull too tightly.

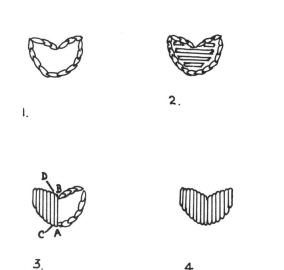

3-81. Satin stitch.

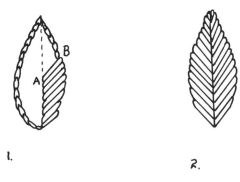

3-82. Slanted satin stitch.

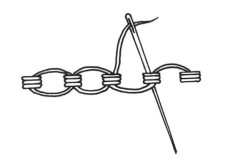

3-83. Guilloche stitch.

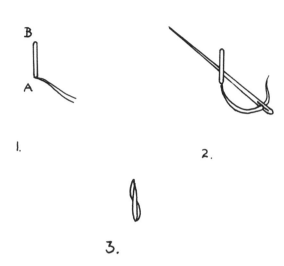

3-84. Twisted satin stitch.

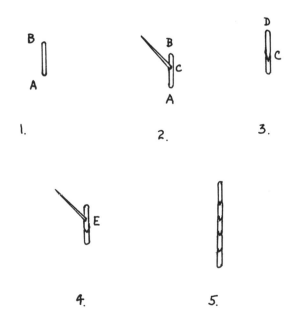

3-85. Split stitch.

77. Split Stitch

This is a versatile and commonly used stitch. It can be worked as a line stitch or as a solid filling with shading. When used in the latter manner, the direction of the stitches will help to suggest shape and movement. The rows of stitching should all go in the same direction. It is the line stitch most commonly used in conjunction with satin stitch or soft shading, under any stitch whose edges need to be raised so that they will not sink down into the surrounding embroidery, or under any stitch that needs a smooth, neat edge (3-85).

a. Needle up at A, down at B on the working line (1).

b. Bring the needle up through stitch AB, splitting the yarn at a point one-third to one-half the way back into this stitch (2).

c. Needle down at D ahead of point B (3). Stitches AB and CD should be of equal length.

d. Needle up at E, splitting the second stitch (4).

e. Continue in this same manner, moving ahead with each stitch, then splitting back into the stitch just made. On a curve the stitches need to be shortened to fit the curve and can be held in position on the line while it is being split. It can also be whipped if desired.

78. Straight Stitch

This stitch is exactly what you might expect, a plain, straight stitch. The various arrangements and groupings of stitches create interesting patterns (3-86). The fern stitch (48) is a good example of this.

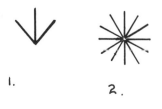

3-86. Straight stitch.

79. Algerian Eye Stitch

This stitch is also used in canvaswork. All eight stitches share the same center (3-87).

    a. Start at one point and work stitches in sequence around the square (1).

    b. (2) shows the stitch in light yarn, with shorter arms of a dark thread placed in between the lighter ones.

80. Turkeywork Stitch

It hardly seems logical that turkeywork should be included in the flat-stitch category, since it has such a definite dimensional quality. But since it is based on the back stitch, it has every right to be included. Turkeywork forms a thick pile, which can be trimmed as high or as low as the situation demands.

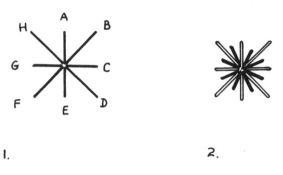

1.   2.

3-87. Algerian eye stitch.

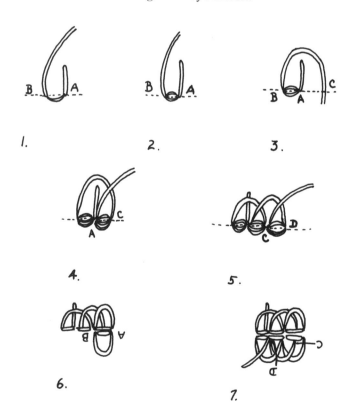

1.   2.   3.

4.   5.

6.   7.

3-88. Turkeywork.

This makes it ideal for working the fur of animals, some insects, puffy centers for flowers, and so on. The method described here is somewhat different from that given in most books. Although it puts more yarn on the back of the fabric, it also puts about twice as much on top where it is most needed, giving a thicker pile (3-88).

    a. Needle down at A, leaving about a 1/2" (12 mm) tail on top, up at B about 1/16" (2 mm) to the left of A (1).

    b. Needle down at A again, up at B, making a tiny back stitch to lock in the first strand (2).

    c. Needle down at C 1/16" (2 mm) to the right of A, leaving about a 1/2" (12 mm) loop on top (3).

    d. Needle up just barely to the right of A, down at C, and up at A again, making a back stitch to lock in this loop (4).

    e. Needle down at D, up just barely to the right of C (5), making the next loop. Then take needle down at D and up at C again, making a back stitch (5). The small up-curved stitches between AB, AC, and CD indicate the part of the back stitch on top of the fabric, and the down-curved lines show the part underneath the fabric. Hold the loops back out of the way with the left thumb while working.

    f. Continue to move ahead about 1/16" with each loop and anchor with a back stitch. Place these back stitches underneath the loops and directly on the working line.

    g. At the end of the line of stitching anchor the last loop and turn work and diagrams upside down.

    h. Holding the loops made on the first row down with the left thumb, work back from left to right (6, 7). Place this row very close to the first row and continue across to the end. The loops made on this second row can also be held down with those of the first row while working.

    i. Stitch back and forth across the area, turning the work at the end of each row until the space is filled. The rows may curve and should follow the contour of the area. Shading can be used with turkeywork, changing and placing the values and colors where needed to give the desired effect. It can be worked with double threads of a fine yarn, resulting in a thicker pile.

    j. Trim off the tops of the loops with sharp scissors. Carefully trim to the desired depth, shaping and sculpturing the pile as the situation demands. Do not cut too close at the outside edges, or the back stitches will show. Cut off only a little at a time, proceeding with caution. It can't be glued back on!

3-89. *Sampler illustrating knotted stitches,*
worked on linen twill with Custom House yarn.

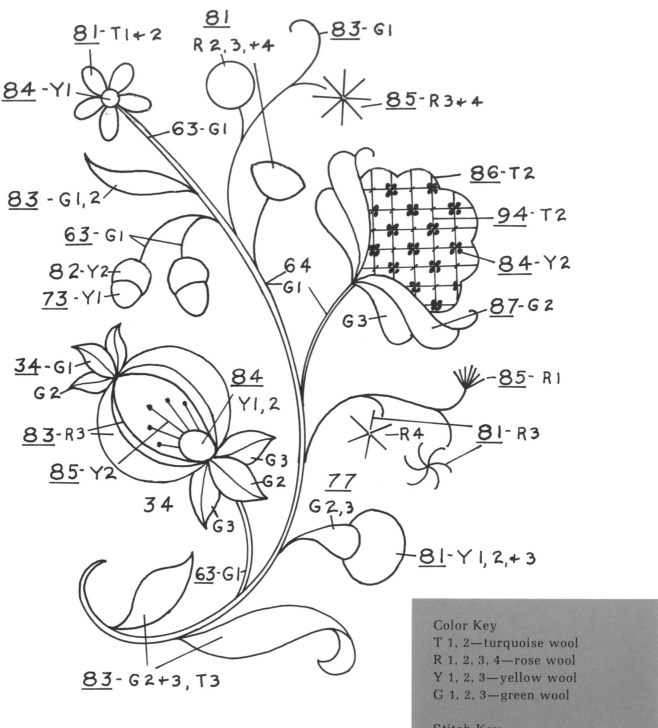

81-T1+2

81
R 2,3,+4

83-G1

84-Y1

85-R3+4

63-G1

86-T2

94-T2

83-G1,2

84-Y2

63-G1

82-Y2
73-Y1

64
G1

87-G2

G3

34-G1
G2

84
Y1,2

85-R1

83-R3

R4

81-R3

85-Y2

G3
G2

34

G3

77
G2,3

81-Y1,2,+3

63-G1

83-G2+3, T3

3-90. *Line drawing and guide for the knotted-stitch sampler.*

Color Key
T 1, 2—turquoise wool
R 1, 2, 3, 4—rose wool
Y 1, 2, 3—yellow wool
G 1, 2, 3—green wool

Stitch Key
63 outline stitch
64 stem stitch
73 satin stitch
81 bullion knot stitch
82 Chinese knot stitch
83 coral knot stitch
84 French knot stitch
85 French knot stitch on a stem
86 Palestrina knot stitch
87 raised knot stitch

81. Bullion Knot Stitch

Because of its textural character this knot stitch is especially effective in embroidery and is extremely versatile as well, fitting into numerous shapes and adapting to varying situations. In order to make it easier to pull the needle through the wound coil, work it with a crewel, millinery, or any other needle with a shank that is about the same size as the eye. The size of the needle is still chosen according to the thickness of the yarn (3-92).

a. Needle up at A, down at B at the other end of the line on which the bullion knot will lie, leaving a fairly long loop of yarn on top of work.

b. Needle halfway up at A again (1).

c. Take the yarn as it comes from point A, wind it around needle enough times so that, when pushed close together on the needle the coil will cover the distance from A to B (2). If the yarn seems to untwist itself as you wind, reverse and wind in the opposite direction. Do not stretch the yarn as you wind.

d. Grasp the coil of yarn on the needle between the left thumb and forefinger (3), hold the part of the needle underneath the work with the right thumb and forefinger (4), and move the needle up and down slightly a few times. This will loosen the coil on the needle a bit, especially if it has been wound too tightly. Do not squeeze the coil with the left hand too much while doing this (4).

e. When the needle moves freely, grasp the point of the needle with the right hand, still holding the coil between the left thumb and forefinger, and pull the needle and yarn all the way through the coil of yarn, wiggling needle slightly as you pull. You may also need to coax the twists of yarn off the back of the needle while pulling through. Draw the yarn in the direction in which the bullion will lie or toward point B (5).

f. Tug gently on the yarn, pushing the coil back toward point A with the point of the needle or with the fingernail until the knot is smooth.

g. Needle down at the end of the knot (6).

3-91. Design worked mostly in knotted stitches, suitable for an eyeglass case.

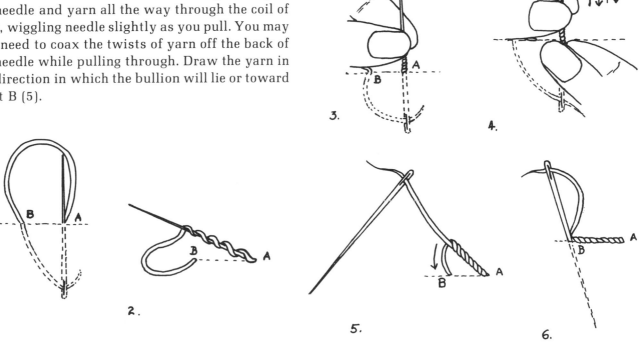

3-92. Bullion knot stitch.

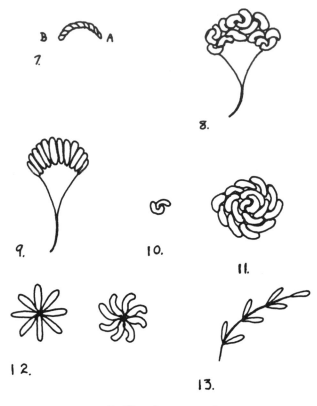

3-92. *Bullion knot stitch.*

h. To make a bullion knot that curls, put more twists on the needle than are needed to cover the distance between points A and B (7). Curled bullion knots may be used in many situations. They may be curved in a random pattern to make a flower head, catkin, or other round shape, fitting one around the other and using several values of a color to achieve either a shaded effect or a random placement of the color values (8). Straight bullions may be worked side by side (9).

i. To make a rosette of curled bullions, start at the center with two curled around each other in a dark value (10). Each bullion in the next row around this center should overlap the previous knot by one-third its length.

j. Continue overlapping, making each row a value lighter.

k. On the outside row use the lightest value, slip the needle out from under the previous row when starting knots, and tuck the other end of the knots in under the last row (11). The length of the knots in each row must be increased and more knots added as you work toward the outside.

l. Small flowers and leaves can be made from straight or curved bullions (12, 13). If you experiment with these knots, you will no doubt invent some additional uses of your own.

82. Chinese Knot Stitch
This knot stitch is somewhat similar to the French knot but has a slight leg or extension. It is firmer, with less tendency to loosen up than the French knot (3-93).

a. Needle up at A. Hold the yarn to the left, then up, slip the needle under the yarn from top to bottom, no fabric, making a loop (1, 2).

b. Tighten up on this loop until it is slightly larger than your thumb, push the loop over to the right so that you can see point A, and take a vertical stitch BC inside the loop to the left of A. The top of the needle is over the loop; the point of the needle goes under the loop (3).

c. Tighten the yarn around the needle (4).

d. Pull through (5). The length of stitch BC will determine the length of the leg. The knot will be positioned at point B or the upper end of the vertical stitch.

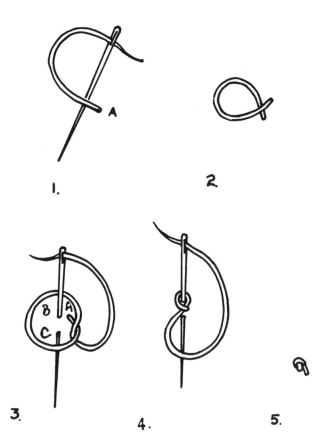

3-93. *Chinese knot stitch.*

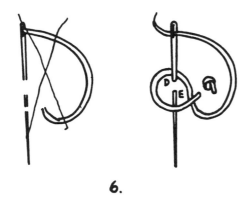

6.

3-93. Chinese knot stitch.

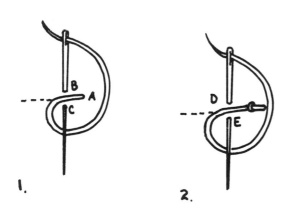

1.

2.

3.

3-94. Coral knot stitch.

e. Loop the yarn as in (1) and work the next knot to the left of the first one, spacing it so that it lies directly beside the first knot (6, 7).

This stitch can be worked without a hoop or with the fabric loose in the hoop. It can also be worked on taut fabric in a hoop by making the loop, inserting the needle halfway down into the fabric, tightening the yarn around the needle, and pulling the needle through to the back. Then bring the needle up for the bottom part of the stitch at C and pull through to the top.

f. These knots may be worked in a single line, in a circle moving toward the center and filling the space completely, or in consecutive rows to solidly fill a larger area. Work all rows in the same direction, staggering the knots so that they fit between knots of the above row. You can shade with these knots if you wish.

83. Coral Knot Stitch
Though the coral knot stitch is most often used as a line stitch, it is also used to fill a space with successive rows, shading by changing values and working partial rows to compensate for widening and narrowing areas. The result is a beautifully textured effect (3-94).

a. Needle up at A at the right end of the working line. Lay the yarn toward the left along the line, circle it down, to the right, then up again (1).

b. Take a vertical stitch BC under the yarn by putting needle down at B just above the line and up at C just below the line, the needle point coming over the looped yarn (1).

c. Pull; when the yarn is almost all the way through, pull straight up to form the knot. This tightens the yarn between knots.

d. Repeat the above steps, working to the.left (2).

e. The spacing is determined by the weight of the yarn and by the finished effect desired. When working successive rows, space the knots so that, when the next row is worked, the knots can be placed between the knots of the previous row.

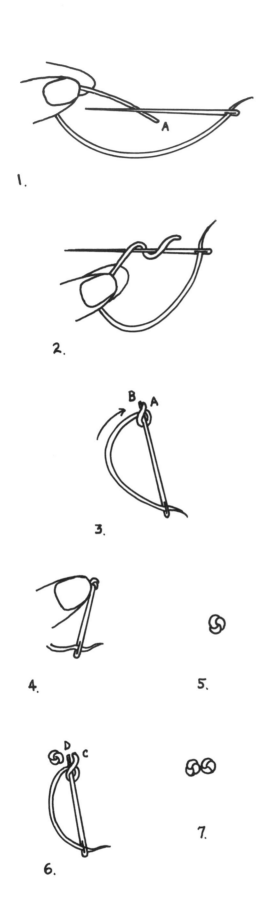

1.

2.

3.

4.

5.

6.

7.

84. French Knot Stitch

The familiar French knot is versatile, fitting into many situations and shapes and creating a textured effect. It can be worked singly, in a line, as a scattered filler, or solidly to completely cover an area. Shading can also be achieved with French knots. A good French knot should be tight, not loopy, and should have a dimple in the center (3-95).

a. Needle up at A. Holding the yarn toward the left between the left thumb and forefinger, place the needle in front of the yarn, needle pointing left (1), and twist the point under, up in back of the yarn, over the top, bringing the point toward yourself, then down under again (2).

b. Slide the twisted yarn toward the point of the needle, holding the end of the right forefinger over the twisted yarn as you slip it toward the point. At the same time swing the point toward A and go down very close to A at B (3).

c. Take the needle only halfway down, tighten the yarn around the needle, then place the left forefinger or thumb directly against the needle over the twist of yarn (4).

d. Pull through, keeping the thumb in position until all yarn is pulled through (5).

e. To make another knot next to the first one, bring the needle up a knot's width away from the last one at C (6).

f. Wrap as before, put the needle down halfway between C and the last knot at D (6). Tighten and pull through. The knots will sit at the point at which the needle goes down.

g. If you prefer to place the needle behind the yarn (8), twist the point of the needle down and under, bringing the point toward yourself, then up and over top of the yarn, ending with the needle pointing away from you (9).

h. Slip the twist of yarn down toward the point of the needle while bringing it around to B, just barely to the right of A (10). Tighten and pull through.

i. To fill an area solidly with French knots, first make a line of knots along the outside line, then fill the space. This will give a neater outline than will working from the inside toward the outer line.

3-95. French knot stitch.

j. To shade with French knots, work a row of the first color value along the outside line, then as many more rows of this same value as are needed. Before starting the next value work a row of knots, leaving spaces the width of a knot between them. Using the next value, fill the spaces left in the last line of knots, then work solid lines until you need to change values again. Continue in the same manner for all values. By working in this manner you are "fingering in" with the different values, using the shading principle to prevent the formation of a banded effect where the different values meet.

To make a larger French knot, either use a heavier yarn or a double strand of a fine one. You can also make the knot larger by using a double wrap of a fine yarn, provided that the resulting knot is tight.

85. French Knot Stitch on a Stem
A French knot on a stem can be used for borders, edgings, and small flowers (3-96).

a. Needle up at A. Wrap the needle around the yarn (1, 2).

b. The needle reenters the fabric at B, the length of AB determined by the length needed for the stem.

c. Tighten the yarn around the needle, hold your finger over the twist against the needle, and pull through (2); (3) shows a flower made with these knots. The shorter stitches may be of a different color or of a strongly contrasting value of the first color.

86. Palestrina Knot Stitch
This handsome knot stitch looks best when worked in a reasonably heavy yarn, double strands of a lightweight yarn, or Perle cotton. It is particularly effective as a border or line stitch and for decorating clothing but can be used to fill spaces as well (3-97).

a. Needle up at A, top of the working line.

b. Needle down at B to the right of the line and below A, up at C directly across from B and to the left of the line. Points A, B, and C should make a small equilateral triangle. A left-handed person will be more comfortable working point B to the left of the line and C to the right.

c. Loop the yarn down and to the right, slip the needle under stitch AB, right to left, no fabric (1).

d. Pull through (2).

e. Looping the yarn as in (1), slip the needle under stitch AB a second time between the loop just made around AB and point B, bringing the needle over the looped yarn (3).

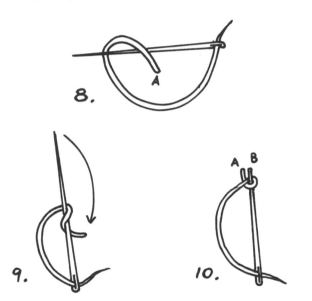

3-95. French knot stitch.

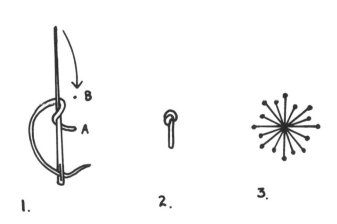

3-96. French knot on a stem.

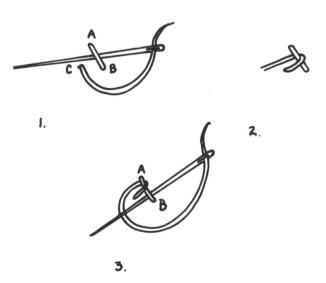

3-97. Palestrina knot stitch.

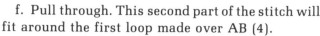

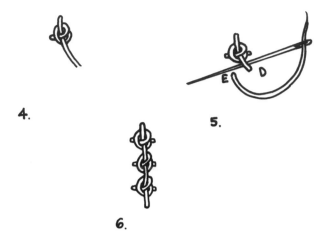

4.

5.

6.

3-97. Palestrina knot stitch.

f. Pull through. This second part of the stitch will fit around the first loop made over AB (4).

g. Needle down at D below B and up at E below C.

h. Loop the yarn down and to the right, slip the needle under the stitch from the first knot to D (5).

i. Pull through, loop the yarn down and to the right again, slip the needle under the same stitch a second time as in (3), and pull through.

j. The weight of the yarn will affect the spacing, but always keep this spacing even once it has been established (6). If this stitch is used to fill an area solidly, space the stitches so that the knots on the next row can be placed between those in the first row.

87. Raised Knot Stitch

Here is how to make the raised knot stitch (3-98).

a. Lay horizontal bars about ⅛″ (3 mm) apart across the area with double yarn, making them taut (1).

b. Needle up at A, loop the yarn down and to the right, slip the needle under the first bar to the left of the yarn, no fabric, needle coming over the loop (2).

c. Pull; when the yarn is almost through, pull it straight up until the knot forms on the bar (3).

d. Loop the yarn down and to the right and repeat on the second bar (4).

e. Continue working one bar at a time, then take the needle down at B, bottom of area (5).

f. Carry the yarn to the top (on the back) and work additional rows next to each other on both sides of the center row, being careful not to crowd the rows too close together. On a curved shape start on the inside of the curve (6).

I.

2.

3.

4.

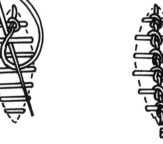

5.

6.

3-98. Raised knot stitch.

3-99. Sampler illustrating couching and laid
stitches, worked on blue British satin in Appleton
yarn and D.M.C. embroidery floss.

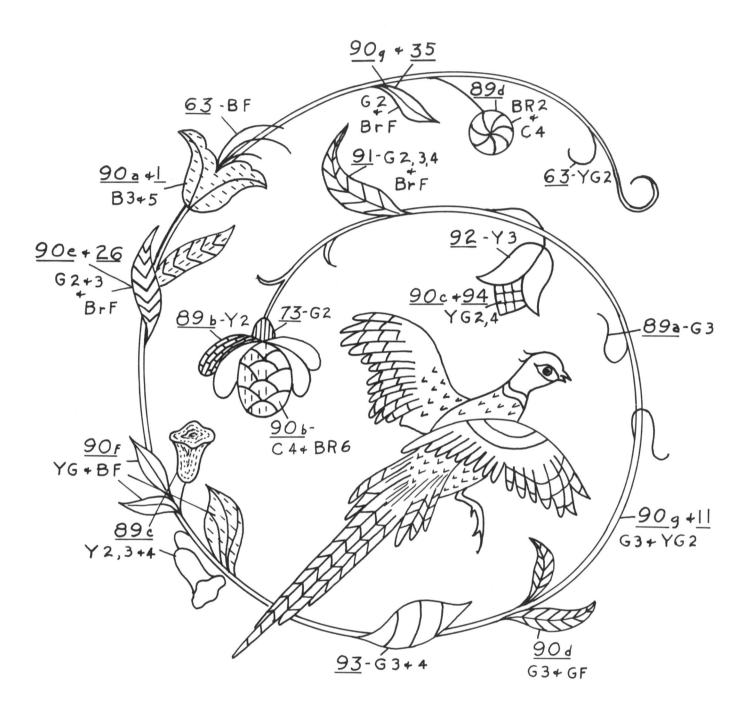

90g + 35

63 - BF

89d BR2 + C4

G 2 + BrF

91 - G 2,3,4 + BrF

63 - YG2

90a + 1 B3 + 5

92 - Y3

90c + 94 YG2,4

90e + 26 G 2 + 3 + BrF

89a - G3

89b - Y2   73 - G2

90f YG + BF

90b - C 4 + BR6

89c Y 2,3 + 4

90g + 11 G3 + YG2

93 - G 3 + 4

90d G3 + GF

3-100. Line drawing and guide for the couching- and laid-stitch sampler.

Color Key

BF—blue floss
BR 2, 3, 5, 6—brown wool
G 2, 3, 4—green wool
C 2, 3, 4—coral wool
Y 2, 3, 4—yellow wool
YG 2, 4—yellow-green wool
BrF—brown floss
GF—green floss
Bl—black wool

The lowest number indicates the lightest value.

Stitch Key

63 outline stitch
73 satin stitch
89a single strand couched, same color
89b single strand bricked, same color
89c single strand couched, same and darker values
89d circular couching stitch
90a horizontal laid strands couched with chain stitch
90b vertical laid strands couched in scale pattern with split stitch
90c laid strands couched with trellis stitch
90d laid strands couched with open fly stitch
90e laid strands couched with open buttonhole stitch
90f laid strands couched with outline stitch
90g multiple strands couched with open chain stitch
91 couched leaf stitch
92 Roumanian couching stitch
93 Bokhara couching stitch

1. Pheasant, body—the body is worked in beige, dull yellows, browns, burnt oranges, black, and white Appleton wool and D.M.C. floss. Work the eye with a French knot in black floss, then split stitch in white floss around it. For the red area around the eye use floss in satin and split stitch, working horizontally. Lay lengthwise strands of black wool on the head, couching each strand as it is laid with the same kind of thread, except for the highlights, which are couched in blue floss. Work the white ring around the neck in satin stitch in white floss. Lay all strands on the adjacent part of the upper body, using different shades and values to give the needed shading. All strands need not be carried the full length. Couch these strands down with brown and white floss, as shown by the V marks.

2. Upper wing—the top-right area is laid and couched with the same thread color. The lower part of the wing is gradually shaded from beige to yellow to burnt orange, then couched as for upper body. Wing feathers are laid in brown and couched one strand at a time on the markings with a contrasting beige wool, blending the ends of the laid strands into the upper wing area. One strand of the beige is carried between the feathers and couched with the same color to separate the feathers.

3. Under body—lay deep tones of burnt orange and brown to give the needed shading and tie down with V marks of dark brown floss.

4. Tail—lay and couch one strand at a time, using muted yellows and a bit of light burnt orange. Couch and separate the feathers with brown wool.

5. Lower wing—follow the same procedure as for the upper wing, working over a line of split stitch on upper wing edge to raise it up over the body stitching.

6. Beak—use straight stitches in beige with brown on the bottom of each section.

7. Feet—lay and couch with the same thread color, using two or three shades of gray wool.

8. Circular stem—lay two (three for the wider portions) strands of green wool, holding them in place with sewing thread, which can be removed later. Couch in this position with a slightly lighter and brighter shade of green, using the open chain stitch.

Use the color picture (C-6) as a guide or find a picture of your own. Match the yarn colors as closely as possible to the picture. This bird requires patience but is worth the effort.

88. Laidwork

In laidwork the yarn lies on top of the fabric and is not carried across on the back, as it is in satin stitch. This not only saves thread but reduces the thickness of the area.

a. Needle up at A at the widest point. Establish the direction in which the threads will lie, whether straight or diagonally (3-101). If the diagonal is chosen, start slightly below widest point.

b. Needle down at B on the opposite side.

c. Needle up at C, as close to B as possible without going in the same hole.

d. Needle down at D very close to A. Continue working back and forth until one side is filled. Then fill the other side, starting at the center. The strands should lie side by side with no material showing between them. These laid strands must be tied down in some manner, such as with simple trellis stitch, detached fly stitch, or lines of outline or chain stitch.

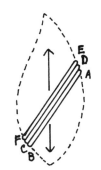

3-101. Laidwork.

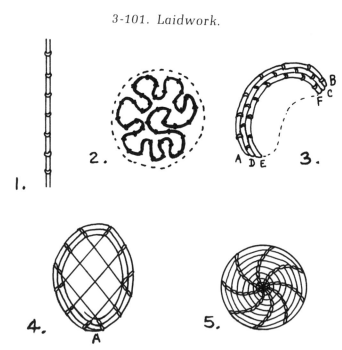

3-102. Some methods of couching a single strand.

89. Couching a Single Strand

Webster defines "couch" in this manner: "to embroider (a design) by laid threads fastened by small stitches at regular intervals." The word is sometimes used to refer to the laid threads as well, but it most often refers only to the tie-down stitch. These couching threads can be the same as the laid ones, or they can differ in either color or texture or both, thereby forming a pattern. The technique of couching lends itself to a great variety of applications.

A single strand of yarn can follow a straight line, a curve, or any shape (3-102) and can be couched at regular intervals (1). A single strand can also be laid to form a free-form or random pattern, wandering in any direction that fits the situation or pleases the stitcher. The thread to be couched is brought up at any point, then wound around to create a random pattern. It can be pinned in place after experimenting with different positions, then couched down at regular intervals with a contrasting thread, using a second needle. This thread is brought up on one side of the laid thread, carried over it, and taken down on the other side, slipping out slightly from under the strand and tucking the needle in and under slightly on the other side. The laid thread can also be maneuvered into position as the couching progresses (2).

Bricked couching is used to completely cover a space.

a. Needle comes up at A (3) and is couched with stitches exactly the width of the laid strand. Their spacing is determined by the weight of the laid and the couching threads and by the shape, but usually it is not greater than 1/4″ (5 mm). If the shape is curved, make the laid thread follow the contour of the area.

b. Needle goes down at B and up at C for next row (3).

c. Couch back in the opposite direction, laying the yarn next to the first row and placing the couching stitches halfway between those on the first row. The second laid strand will lie closer to the first if the couching stitch comes up on the outside of the strand being worked and goes down next to the first couched strand, slanting the needle slightly under it. By changing the color value of the couching thread and the closeness of the stitches a shaded effect can be produced.

d. Continue working back and forth, following the bricking pattern until the space is filled. If you want the couching stitches to be unobtrusive, use the same thread as for the laid stitches. If you want the bricking pattern to show, use a contrasting thread.

In order to create a definite pattern with couching stitches, mark the desired pattern on the fabric. Use one needle for the yarn being laid and another for the couching thread. Use a contrasting thread for the couching so that the pattern made by the stitches will be obvious.

a. Bring thread to be laid up at A and make a couching stitch wherever the laid thread crosses a marking. The direction of the couching stitches should follow the lines of the pattern.

b. The laid thread can be carried back and forth across the area (3), or it may continue around the shape (4).

A circle can be worked in the same manner. Mark the lines as shown (5) or in any other pattern.

a. Bring the yarn for the laid strand up in the center and the couching thread on one line at center, using a second needle.

b. Carry the laid thread around in a circular direction, tying down wherever it crosses a marked line. When completed, the couching stitches will show up as the pattern, especially if a contrasting thread is used.

c. On the outside tuck the needle of laid thread in under the last round.

90. Couching Multiple Strands

Any number of strands of yarn may be laid down to follow any line or pattern (3-103). There are many ways to tie these down, such as with straight (1), buttonhole (2), open chain (3), or cross-stitch (4). If these laid strands must accurately follow a line, they will be easier to handle if they are first held in position with stitches of regular sewing thread, which can be removed later. Be careful not to split these basting or temporary stitches while the couching is worked.

Leaves or other shapes can be covered with laid strands, then tied down in a variety of ways either with yarn or with contrasting types of threads. A leaf of vertical laid strands can be tied with open buttonhole stitch worked on a slant (5). Diagonal strands can be held in place with curved lines of outline stitch (6). Vertical strands can also be tied with open fly stitch (7) or with trellis stitch (8). These are but a few of the possibilities. The laid strands can be the same value or graduated to give a shaded effect. An area can be covered with vertical laid strands tied down to simulate a scalelike pattern (9). This stitching could be worked in chain, outline, split, or any other line stitch.

5.

6.

7.

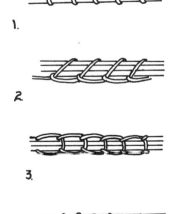

1.

2.

3.

4.

9.

8.

3-103. Some methods of couching multiple strands.

91. Couched Leaf

An interesting treatment for a leaf is to couch one strand of yarn at a time with a contrasting thread so that the couching stitches form the veins. First mark the center and side veins on the fabric. Use two needles, one for the laid threads and one for the couching. The color and value of the couching thread should contrast sufficiently with the values used in the laidwork so that it can be readily seen but should not form so stark a contrast as to dominate the leaf (3-104).

a. Needle with the couching thread up at A and down at B. If the leaf curves, adjust the length of this thread so that it exactly fits the center vein. Couch it down with the same thread at the points where the side veins meet in the center, working down from the top toward the base of the leaf (1).

b. Using the darkest value for the laidwork in the second needle, slip the needle out from under the center vein at C and couch this strand down at each vein that it crosses. Couch from the outside of the laid strand back toward the first laid strand, placing the second part of the couching stitch in the same hole made by the last couching stitch. If the couching stitches are too wide, they will space the laid strands apart and allow fabric to show between them.

c. The laid strand goes down at D, slipping in under the center vein (2).

d. Slant the needle with the laid thread out from under the laid strand at E on the other side of the vein. Couch down the second side and slant the needle under at F (2).

e. The next laid thread comes up at G, is couched up that side at each vein line, then goes down at H. The strand from I to J goes down the other side of the leaf (3). These partial lines are used to shape the laid strands to the outside contour of the leaf.

f. Continue in the same manner until the entire leaf area is filled (4).

g. This type of leaf usually looks better if only token amounts of the darker values are used—just enough to give sufficient contrast. Leave enough space to work in all the other values, using them in sequence as you move toward the outside edge. The outside strands run completely from the base to the tip and from the tip to the base of the leaf.

h. The value of the couching thread can either remain the same for the entire leaf or be changed to a lighter value as the laid strands become lighter. The laid thread is kept free and is not taken down at the far end while couching is in progress so that it can be moved aside, making it easier to see where the couching stitches should be placed. Adjust the tension on the laid thread after all the couching stitches are completed for that particular strand.

92. Roumanian Couching Stitch

In this version the laid and the couching stitches are made with the same thread. The New England laid stitch is worked in the same manner, except that it usually uses a longer tie-down. The stitch can be worked from left to right or from top to bottom. It can also be done from right to left, but the result is not as smooth (3-105).

a. Mark guidelines on the fabric to follow when making the couching stitches. This assures a neater appearance for the finished stitch.

b. Needle up at A on the left side, yarn looped down, needle down at B on the opposite line, and up at C on the right-hand guideline (1).

c. Pull through (2).

d. Yarn up, needle down at D on the left guideline, tucking the point of the needle slightly under strand

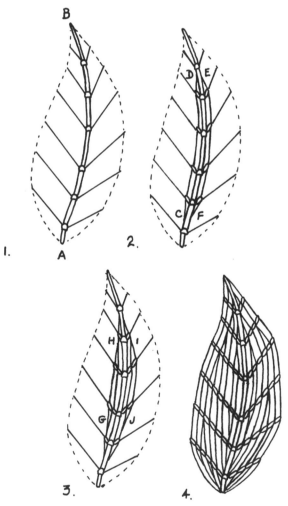

3-104. Couched leaf.

AB, and up again at E directly under A (3).

e. Pull through (4).

f. Yarn looped down, needle down at F directly below B, and up at G on right guideline just barely under C (5).

g. Pull through (6). The needle will go down at H, tucking in below D to complete the second couching stitch.

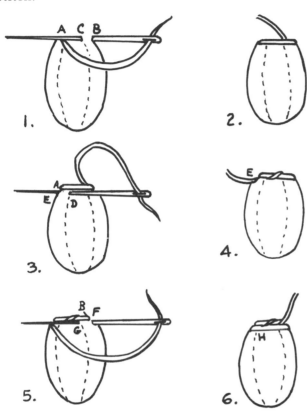

3-105. Roumanian couching stitch.

h. Continue working down or across the area until it is filled. If the area is more curved on one side than on the other, an occasional fill-in stitch may be needed. Bring the needle up on that line and tuck the point of the needle in at the nearer end of the last tie-down stitch. Then make the next complete stitch. The pattern made by the stitch will not be disrupted, and you will be able to swing around the curve more easily.

i. The width of the couching stitch is optional and can be changed to fit the situation. Longer couching stitches usually allow the laid strands to lie closer together, giving better coverage of the material.

93. Bokhara Couching Stitch

This stitch is somewhat similar to Roumanian couching but uses several small tie-down stitches to hold down a long laid strand. These tie-downs can form a definite pattern, following guidelines marked on the fabric (3-106).

a. Needle up at A on the left side, yarn held up, down at B on outside line, and up at C just to the right of the first guideline (1).

b. Pull through; with yarn held down, put the needle down at D above the strand AB just barely to the left of the guideline and bring the needle up at E just below A (2).

c. Pull through. This makes a tie-down stitch over the first guideline.

d. Needle down at F and up at G just to the right of the guideline (3). Strand EF should be just under AB with no fabric showing between them. Lay the yarn in this position to find the location of point F. Pull through.

e. Needle down at H just to the left of the guideline and up at I just below E (4).

f. Continue as with the first two strands, tying down wherever the laid thread crosses a guideline and placing the ends of the laid strands along the outside edges of the shape (5).

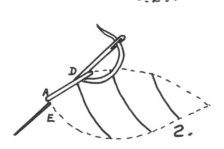

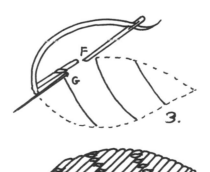

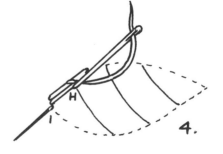

3-106. Bokhara couching stitch.

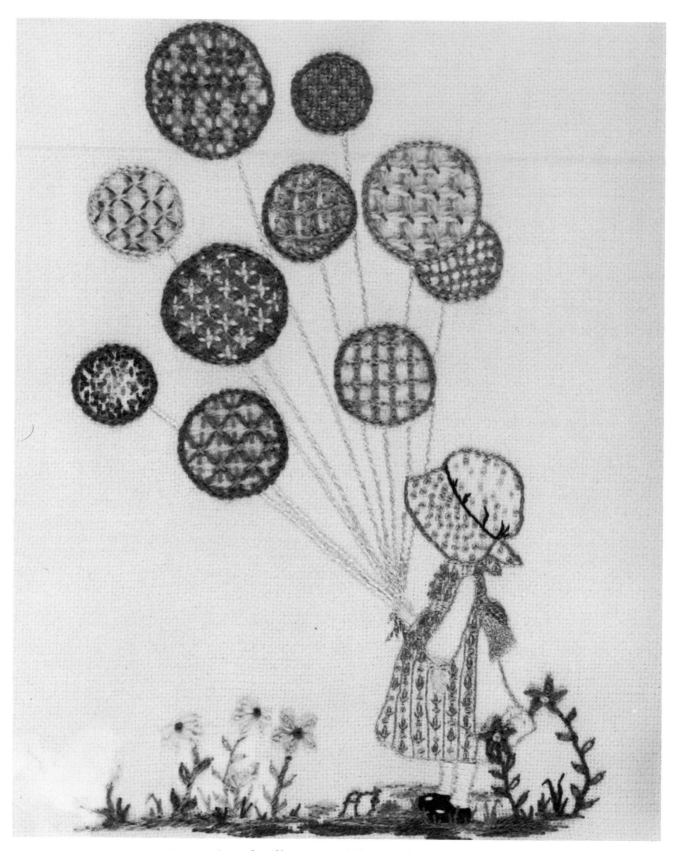

3-107. Sampler illustrating filler stitches, worked
on synthetic fabric with Appleton yarn, D.M.C.
embroidery floss, and #8 Perle cotton.

Filler stitches provide a means of balancing out solidly worked areas by giving lightness and variety to the finished appearance of the design. They technically belong in the category of couching and laid stitches, but, since they play such a specialized role in embroidery, they have been given a section of their own. The possible filling variations are almost endless. The majority are based on the simple trellis or squared filler stitch; others consist of evenly spaced, scattered, detached stitches. All need to be outlined in some manner and must be worked on a hoop.

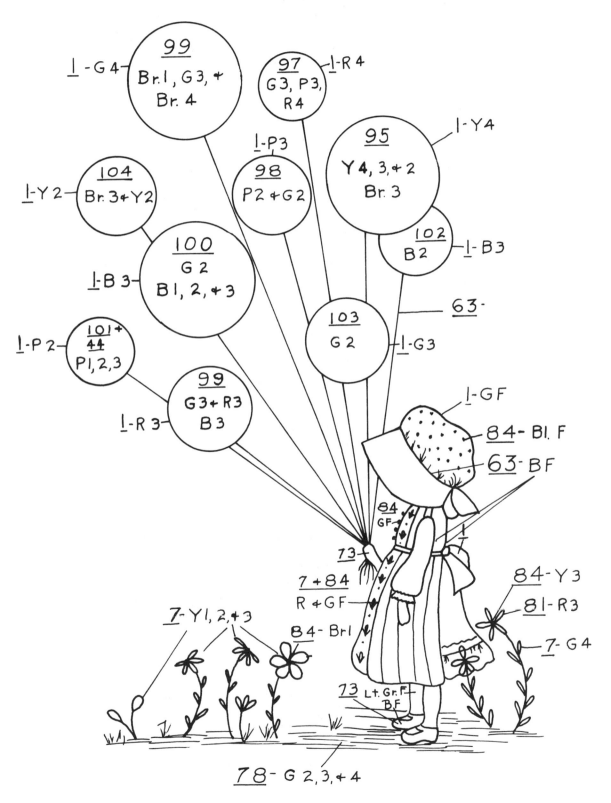

3-108. *Line drawing and guide for the filler-stitch sampler.*

Color Key
R 3, 4—red wool
Br 1, 3—brown wool
G 2, 3, 4—green wool
B 1, 2, 3, 4—blue wool
P 1, 2, 3—purple wool
Y 1, 2, 3, 4—yellow wool
BF—black floss
BlF—blue floss
Lt GF—light gray floss
RF, GF—red, green floss
The lowest number indicates the lightest value.

Stitch Key
1 chain stitch
7 detached chain stitch
7 slipped detached chain stitch
63 outline stitch
73 satin stitch
78 straight stitch
81 bullion knot stitch
84 French knot stitch
95 battlemented filler stitch
97 checkerboard filler stitch
98 outline—slipped detached chain stitch
99 overlaid filler—tied with cross-stitch
99 overlaid filler—woven tie-down stitch
100 satin filler stitch
101 shaded seed stitch
102 web stitch
103 woven chain stitch
104 whipped filler stitch

No particular working sequence is needed except for the flowers in front of the dress and the grass over the shoes, which should be done last.

94. Simple Trellis or Squared Filler Stitch

Here is how to work this basic filler stitch (3-109).

a. Strands of evenly spaced yarn are laid in one direction over the area to be covered. These may be vertical, horizontal, or diagonal (1), following the letters A, B, C, D, and so on.

b. Lay strands in the opposite direction, perpendicular to the first set and with the same spacing (2). It is better to train the eye through practice to achieve even spacing than it is to attempt to mark these lines on the fabric. It is more difficult than it may seem to mark them accurately. If you find that the spacing is not satisfactory, it cannot be changed because of the markings. Some people have a more accurate eye than others for this type of work. If you cannot master the technique, use a small strip of index card the width of the space that you are working as a spacer or guide to measure the distance between the ends of the strands (3). If the area has both wide and narrow parts, lay the first strand in a reasonably wide section. It is easier to make the next one parallel if the eye has a fairly long line to follow. Do not lay any strands directly on the outside lines, as they will be stitched in some manner later.

c. The trellis may be tied down in any number of ways, some of which are: half-cross-stitch (4), cross-stitch (5), cross-stitch with French knot in center of square (6), detached chain with French knots (7), and detached chain with satin stitch (8).

95. Battlemented Filler Stitch

Use three or four values of a color, or strands of different colors may be used to unify an area of the design (3-110).

a. Lay the darkest value first, working all vertical strands, then all horizontal or perpendicular ones (1). With next darkest value lay all vertical, then all horizontal strands so that they just touch one side of first set, no fabric showing between (2). Repeat with other values, laying them in sequence.

b. Tie down only the last set of strands with a half-cross-stitch, using a contrasting color of yarn. The other layers will be held in place by the top one (3).

c. Be sure that the spacing is such that, after all values are laid, an open area is visible in each square. A dimensional effect is produced by the change from light values on top to the dark ones underneath.

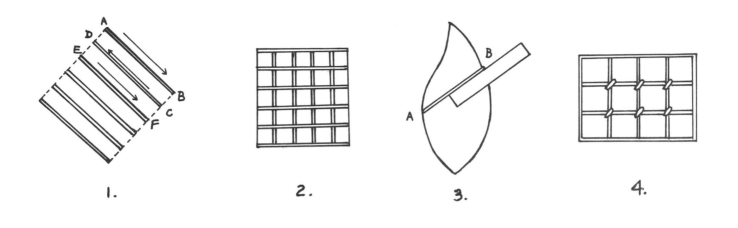

1.   2.   3.   4.

5.   6.   7.   8.

3-109. Simple trellis or squared filler stitch.

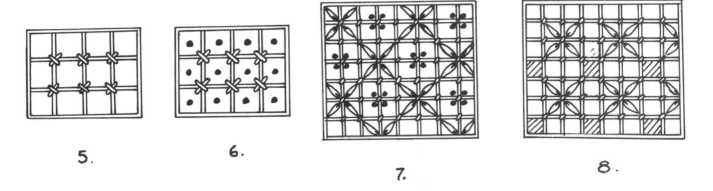

1.   2.   3.

3-110. Battlemented filler stitch.

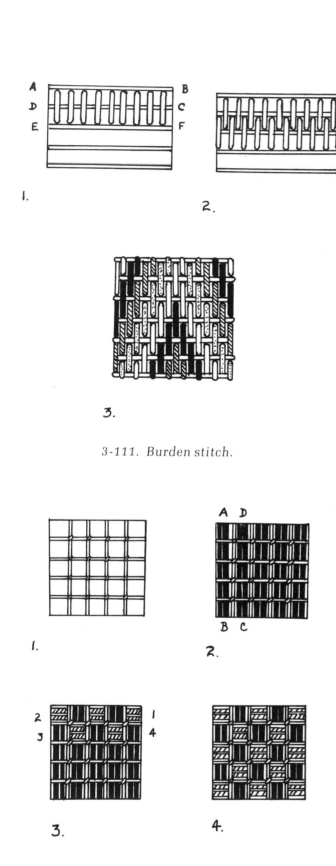

3-111. Burden stitch.

3-112. Checkerboard filler stitch.

96. Burden Stitch

When worked with stitches that are close together, an entirely different effect is apparent than when the stitches are spaced apart to give a lacy look. Shading can be achieved with the close version, or Florentine stitch can be simulated by judicious positioning of yarn values (3-111).

a. Lay horizontal parallel bars AB, CD, EF, and so on slightly less than 1/4" (5 mm) apart (1).

b. Work vertical stitches over CD, with ends of stitches just touching the edges of AB and EF and leaving a space the width of the yarn between the stitches (1).

c. The stitches of the next row are staggered between those of the first row and just touch the edges of the bars between which they extend (2).

d. Continue until all the space is filled, using half stitches on the ends as needed.

e. If you are shading with this stitch, place the various values so as to give the desired effect; (3) shows a simulation of Florentine stitch.

97. Checkerboard Filler Stitch

Use this filler in a reasonably small area. It is effective but can be tedious in a large area, since the squares cannot be very large (3-112).

a. Lay a simple trellis base, tying down with the same yarn and with as small a half-cross-stitch as possible. The spacing on the trellis should be such that two strands of yarn will fill the space (1).

b. With a double strand of a contrasting color of yarn and a tapestry needle, come up at A, slip the needle under the trellis to the other end, pull through, needle down at B (2).

c. Repeat with the needle up at C, slide the needle under the trellis and down at D (2). If you have made the squares the proper size but find it hard to cover fabric, use a single strand, laying the two strands separately and passing through each lane twice.

d. Using another contrsting yarn whose color value is sufficiently different from the first so that a definite contrast is apparent, work in the opposite direction as follows:

(1) Needle up at 1 (3), weave over the strands laid in previous step in one square, under in the next square, and so on. Always keep the trellis on top by working under it at all times. Down at 2 at the end of the row.

(2) Needle up at 3 (3). Weave back in the next lane, working over yarn in a square directly next to one that went under on the previous row.

(3) Continue until all of the area has been worked in both directions (4).

98. Outline with Slipped, Detached Chain Stitch

Any of the line stitches may be used in place of laid strands for the lines of a trellis. They may be straight or curved. The latter will carry out the rounded feeling when used for a circle or oval shape. In this example a circle with curved rows of outline stitch was used. Slipped, detached chain stitches were made in the lower corners (3-113). Other detached stitches, as well as other line stitches, may be substituted.

99. Overlaid Filler Stitch

This is a beautiful filler that makes a lacy pattern. There are at least three variations in the manner in which it may be tied. It should not be worked in a small area, as the effect of the stitch is completely lost if worked too closely or too small (3-114).

a. Lay strands of yarn first in one direction, then in the opposite direction. These squares should measure 3/16" to 1/4" (5 mm) on a side. Use a guide if necessary to be sure that the squares are exact—the success of the next step depends upon this. If you have difficulty making the second set exactly perpendicular to the first, use the corner of a card to establish the first strand in the opposite direction and line the others up with that strand (1).

b. Using a contrasting color, lay diagonal strands in both directions, crossing the intersections of the first set (2). The color used for these lines will be more obvious than that used for the first set. Take this fact into consideration when selecting your colors.

c. Three methods for tying this filler down are as follows:

(1) Make a cross-stitch at the points where all eight strands intersect. Use a contrasting color and split the yarn of the lower layer when making the crosses (3).

(2) Tie with a cross-stitch at points where top-layer strands intersect (4).

(3) Weave around the intersections of eight strands, taking the yarn over the top layer and under the bottom layer. The needle goes back down in the same hole in which it came up. Do not pull this weaving too tight (5, 6).

3-113. Outline with slipped, detached chain stitch.

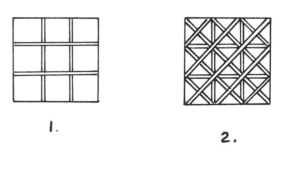

1.

2.

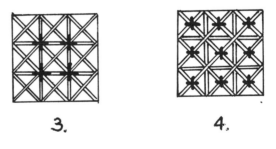

3.

4.

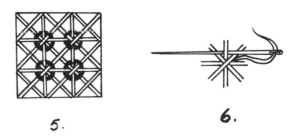

5.

6.

3-114. Overlaid filler stitch.

100. Satin Filler Stitch

This is another beautiful filler that rewards the patience necessary for working it. As with the overlaid filler, do not work it in too small a space. Shading can be achieved by varying the values of the yarn as the squares are filled (3-115).

a. Lay two parallel strands of yarn, leaving a space equal to the width of the yarn between them. Use a guide if necessary to assure even spacing (1).

b. Fill the blocks or diamonds with a satin stitch in a contrasting color, first working the middle stitch, filling to one corner or side, then returning to the middle and working to the opposite corner or side (2).

c. The ends of the satin stitch should fall exactly at the line of yarn, outlining that block.

d. With another contrasting color bring the needle up at A, slightly within the satin stitch. Place the point of the needle inside the intersecting point of the four strands (3), separating them from each other, since the satin stitch tends to push them together. Pull back toward A very slightly with the point of the needle and go down.

e. Needle up at B opposite in the satin stitch, pull back a bit, then take the needle down (3).

f. Repeat for the other two corners to complete one intersection. A speck of background fabric should show in the center of these four tie-down stitches. The strands of the trellis should lie directly over the ends of the satin stitch. This can be controlled to some degree with the tie-down stitches.

g. The contrast between the trellis, satin, and tie-down stitches should be sufficient for good separation, but not so strong that each element stands out in relief; (4) shows the completed filler.

101. Scattered Filler Stitch

This group consists of a variety of detached or individual stitches scattered over an open area. The possibilities are almost endless, including cross-, detached chain, fly, French knot, seeding, slipped detached chain, and tête-de-boeuf stitches (3-116). Though they do not fit the scattered classification, line stitches with various detached stitches are also useful as fillers. A few are illustrated.

102. Web Stitch

The beauty of the web stitch as a filler is its light, airy, and slightly irregular pattern. It also relieves the inevitable square pattern of most fillers (3-117).

a. If there is a wide portion in the area to be filled, begin there. Needle up at A, loop the yarn as for buttonhole and work a row of open buttonhole stitches across the area (1).

b. At the other side take the needle down at B on the line, actually making another stitch. Note that no yarn is placed on the outside lines. The stitches are slightly irregular in shape, as this is part of the charm of the stitch (2).

c. Needle up at C on the right, outside line, below B, looping the yarn toward the left (3).

d. Slip the needle, top to bottom, under the lower strand of the stitch above, needle entering the fabric slightly below it at D and emerging at E below D (3).

e. Pull through, bringing the needle over the looped yarn. Since the needle goes a bit below the bottom of the previous stitch, this lower strand is pulled down from the straight position that it formerly occupied (4).

f. Work across, slipping under each stitch above in the same manner, taking the needle down at F and up at G, ready to start the trip back (5).

g. Continue working back and forth; on the last row use "faked" stitches.

h. Needle up on the bottom line at H, slip the needle under the bottom of the stitch above and into the fabric a bit below and pull through (6). Dots on the bottom line indicate the placement of the other bottom stitches. As the area narrows, simply drop off and do not use the end stitches.

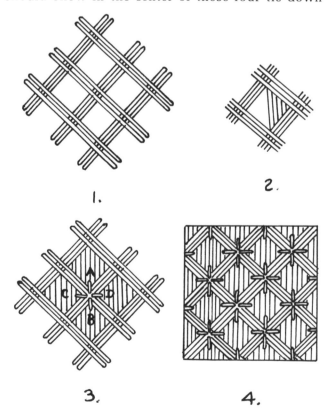

1.   **2.**

3.   **4.**

3-115. Satin filler stitch.

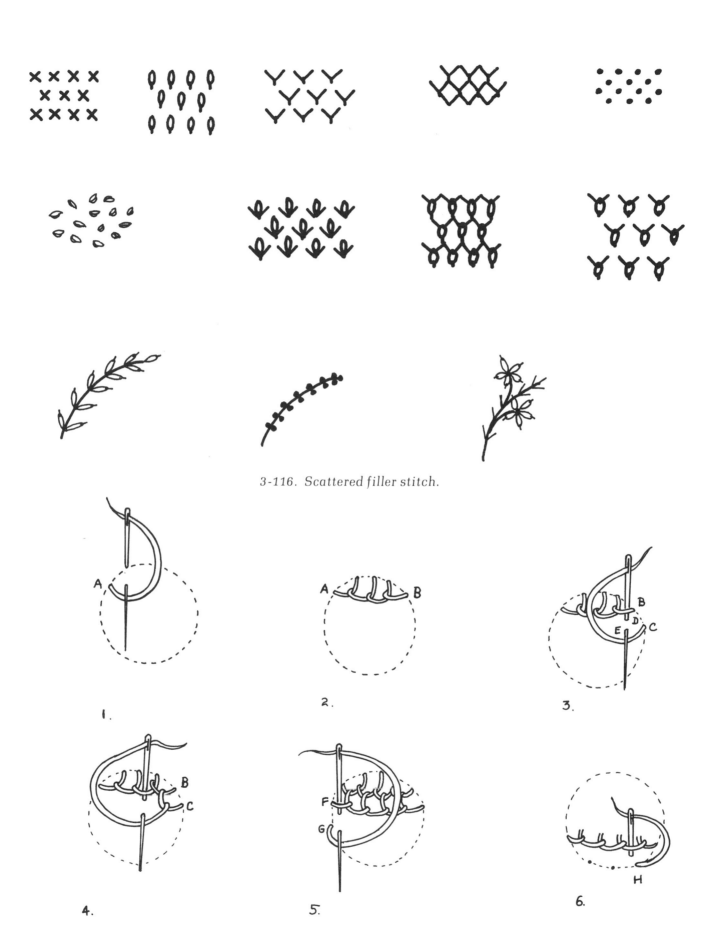

3-116. Scattered filler stitch.

1.

2.

3.

4.

5.

6.

3-117. Web stitch.

3-118. Woven chain stitch.

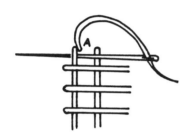

I.

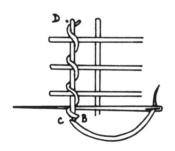

2.

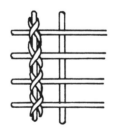

3.

3-119. Whipped filler stitch.

103. Woven Chain Stitch

Here is how to work the woven chain stitch (3-118).

a. First work rows of chain stitch in one direction.

b. When stitching the rows in the opposite direction, work over the first line of chain, under the next line, then over, and so on.

c. On the return trip work over the stitches that went under before and under those that went over. A weaving pattern results. Squares may be filled with detached stitches or in some other manner if desired.

104. Whipped Filler Stitch

Here is how to work the whipped filler stitch (3-119).

a. Work vertical strands, then horizontal ones, as for the simple trellis (94).

b. Using a contrasting color and a tapestry needle, come up at A, just to the right of the first vertical strand.

c. Slip the needle, right to left, under the vertical strand between point A and the first two cross strands, no fabric (1).

d. Pull through and continue to bottom, working down one row at a time. The needle goes down at B just to the right of the vertical strand (2).

e. Needle up at C just to the left of the same vertical strand, weave back up to top, needle going from right to left (2). Needle down at D; (3) shows one line completed.

f. Repeat for all vertical strands.

g. Horizontal bars are also whipped in the same manner as are the vertical ones.

3-120. Sampler illustrating weaving stitches, worked on off-white British satin with Appleton yarn, D.M.C. embroidery floss, #8 Perle cotton, and linen thread.

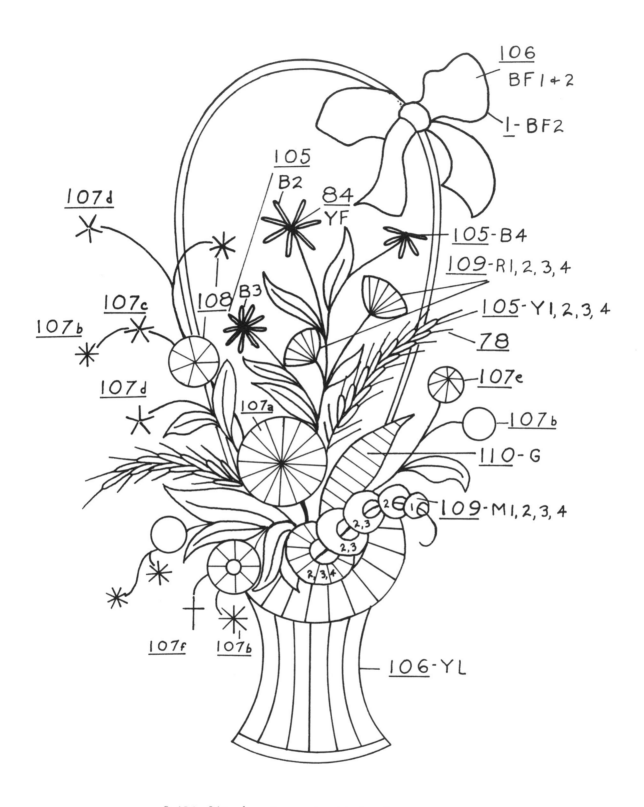

106
BF I + 2

I - BF 2

107d

105
B2

84
YF

105 - B4

109 - R1, 2, 3, 4

108 B3

107c

107b

105 - Y1, 2, 3, 4

78

107d

107e

107a

107b

110 - G

109 - M1, 2, 3, 4

2, 3

2, 3

2, 3, 4

107f   107b

106 - YL

3-121. Line drawing and guide for the weaving-
stitch sampler.

Color Key

R 1, 2, 3, 4—rose wool
B 1, 2, 3, 4—blue wool
M 1, 2, 3, 4—mauve wool
G 1, 2, 3—two families of green wool
YF—yellow floss
GP—green Perle cotton
BP—blue Perle cotton
YL—yellow linen
BF 1, 2—blue floss
Y 1, 2, 3, 4—yellow wool
The lowest number indicates the lightest value.

Stitch Key

  63, 64, 65 outline, stem, and whipped stitches
  78   straight stitch
  84   French knot stitch
105   needle weaving stitch
106   surface darning stitch
107a circular whipped spider stitch
107b circular whipped spider stitch, whorled
107c circular whipped spider stitch, 6 spokes
107d circular whipped spider stitch, 5 spokes
107e circular whipped spider stitch, eccentric
      center
107f God's eye stitch
108   circular woven spider stitch
109   crescent whipped spider stitch
110   horizontal spider stitch

1. Bow—four strands of medium blue floss are laid in one direction, then woven in opposite direction with four strands of light blue floss. The entire bow is outlined with one row of chain stitch worked with one strand of medium blue floss.

2. Basket—yellow linen thread. Vertical laid strands are held in curved position with sewing thread while the weaving is done. This thread can then be removed. A few stitches of darker yellow wool under the edge of the rim add shadowing. The basket handle and base are worked with three strands of braided linen thread, then couched into place with matching sewing thread. Work the body of the basket before the rim of the basket.

3. Leaves—all leaves are worked in closed fly and fishbone stitches in varying shades of green.

4. Stems—outline, whipped outline, or stem stitch.

5. Large circular spider—green in center, then M1, B4, B1, B4, B1. It is outlined with Palestrina knot stitch in the blue Perle (#8).

6. Horizontal spider—shaded from dark in center to the lightest on the outside, then outlined with Portuguese stem stitch in #8 green Perle.

7. Circular spiders—mixed values of rose, mauve, and blue, arranged so as to balance colors.

8. Wheat—needle weaving stitch with darkest value at base, working to lightest at tip, using four values. When putting this design on fabric, mark only the spokes of the spiders.

105. Needle Weaving Stitch

A completed bar of needle weaving stitch is wider and of a different texture than the bullion knot stitch, which is often used in somewhat similar situations. It can be used to make flower petals, small leaves, and wheat grains (3-122).

a. Lay two strands of yarn next to each other but not in the same holes (1).

b. Needle up at A just barely above and between the two strands. Using a blunt needle, slip it between the two strands from the center, going under one strand toward the outside (2).

c. Pull through. Slip the needle, center to the outside, under the other strand (3).

d. Pull through, holding the yarn up toward the starting point.

e. Repeat the last two steps, alternating sides and always starting the needle at the center and going toward the outside; (4) shows the beginning of the next stitch.

f. As the needle is placed in position for each stitch, push back against the previous stitches so that they are packed tightly.

g. Place the needle in between the strands before pulling the last stitch tight, or it will be difficult to insert it.

h. When strands are completely filled, take the needle down at B (5).

106. Surface Darning or Weaving Stitch

This stitch could just as easily be included in the section on filler stitches, but, since this entire section deals exclusively with weaving, it is placed here. Some books call this stitch pattern darning; this version is plain, ordinary sock darning for those of us who are old enough to remember (3-123).

a. Lay parallel strands of yarn (double strands of fine yarn) in one direction, leaving spaces between them equal to the width of the yarn.

b. With a contrasting color or value of yarn and a blunt needle come up at A, about the middle of the area being filled. Weave over and under the strands laid in first step (1).

c. Needle down at B, pull through, making sure that this strand is lying straight, not in a curved position (1).

d. Needle up at C, width of yarn away from B.

e. Weave back in the opposite direction, going under the strands that the needle went over in the first step and over those that it went under (2), needle down at D. The stitches are separated slightly in the diagram for clarity.

f. Continue working back and forth, pushing very gently with the needle against the previous rows to keep them straight. Do not crowd the strands of this second color or value too much, or the color of the first step will be partially obscured. All the fabric should be covered.

g. When one side of the shape is filled, start at the center and work to the other side.

h. The first set of strands can be spaced further apart for a different finished appearance, as in the basket in the weaving sampler.

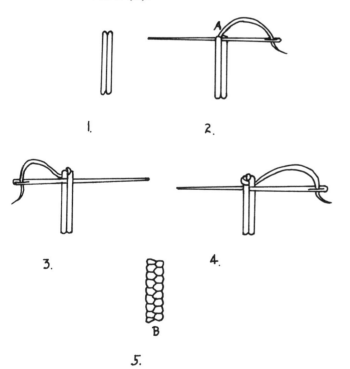

3-122. Needle weaving stitch.

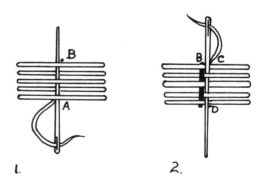

3-123. Surface darning or weaving stitch.

WHIPPED SPIDER STITCHES

Spider stitches are a form of needle weaving stitch, whether they are whipped or woven. The whipped spider stitch is extremely versatile, since it can be adapted to so many shapes and situations. It creates a texture and dimension that is rivaled by only a few other stitches. The yarn can be changed as the spider stitches are being worked, making it possible to shade them.

107. Circular Whipped Spider Stitch

This stitch can be worked over an even or an uneven number of spokes. Since it is easier to lay an even number of spokes with regular spacing, this is the procedure most often used. Mark the center of the circle (3-124).

a. For laying the spokes use double strands of fine yarn and single strands of heavy yarn. Needle up at A and down in center, up at B and down in center, and so on, using the same hole, until all spokes are laid (1). If the spider is being worked where a line marks the perimeter, extend spokes beyond the line to ensure that it will be covered when the spider is completed. Use a tight tension on the spokes. Tie off securely on the back. Cut off one strand if double yarn was used, leaving the other strand attached to use for whipping. When whipping is completed, a bit of the color used for laying the spokes will show in the center. Take this fact into consideration when selecting colors and lay the spokes in the same color that you plan to use for the center.

b. Whipping should be done with a single strand, heavy or fine, and may be either the same color as was used on spokes or a different color.

c. Needle up as close to the center as possible and between any two spokes (2). Change to a tapestry needle.

d. Hold the yarn taut over the center, slip the needle from right to left under the two spokes on either side of the point where yarn emerges, no fabric (2).

e. Pull through and hold back over center.

f. Slip the needle under the next two spokes, again to the right and left of the point where yarn emerges (3).

g. Pull through and back over the center, always holding this yarn to keep it taut. Each time the needle goes under two spokes, it wraps the right one and puts the yarn in position to wrap the next spoke.

h. Continue to repeat the above steps, moving ahead one spoke at a time and turning the hoop as work progresses around the circle (4).

i. After the first complete row, push back gently with the needle against the part that has already been whipped. When the spokes are almost filled, place the tip of the blunt needle next to a spoke and, using gentle pressure, draw the needle from the center to the outside of the spoke. Repeat for all spokes. This procedure spreads the wrapped threads evenly on the spokes and prevents a heavy buildup of yarn.

j. Add as many more rounds as are needed to fill the spokes.

k. On the last wrap go under only one spoke, the one to the right, then tuck the needle in just ahead of the next spoke and tie off; (5) shows a completed spider.

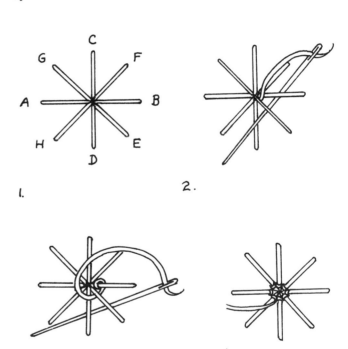

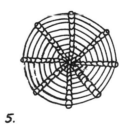

3-124. *Circular whipped spider stitch.*

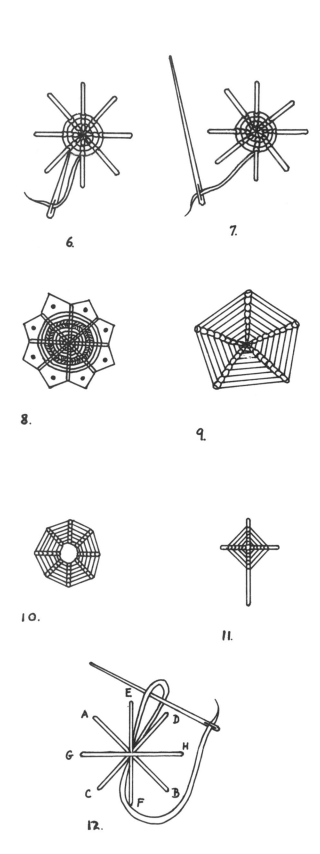

l. Place the needle flat between spokes, press, and wiggle it back and forth. This flattens the portion between the spokes and sharpens the ridges.

m. The color or value of the yarn may be changed at any point, though it looks better if the change is made after a complete round. To change yarn, take the needle down next to the wound portion and just ahead of the next unwound spoke (6). With the new yarn bring the needle up just to the left of an unwound spoke and proceed as before (7). When planning colors for circular whipped spider stitches, keep in mind the fact that stark and sudden color or value changes will result in more interesting spider stitches.

n. The possible variations on the circular whipped spider stitch are almost endless. The ends of the spokes can be left unwhipped. French knots can be put at the ends of the spokes or between them; the finished spider can be outlined with any line stitch, smooth or textured; angled satin stitches can be worked around the perimeter, extending out from the ends of the spokes (8); (9) shows a whipped spider worked on five spokes; (10) shows a circular spider with spokes that do not meet in the center—this open center can be filled with French knots or satin stitch or left open; (11) illustrates a spider worked on four spokes, one longer than the others—this is often referred to as a God's eye.

o. An alternate method for laying the spokes, which does not result in as neat a center, is to lay the yarn all the way across the circle from A to B, C to D, and so on. Before starting to whip bring the needle up at the center and slip it under the crossed yarn to other side of center. Loop the yarn, pass the needle through the loop, and pull up (12). Whip as directed above. This method results in a more raised or puffy spider.

p. When working very small spiders, lay the spokes with a single thread and, instead of making the tension taut, leave them very slightly relaxed. As the spider is whipped and the yarn pulled tight, the spokes will curve slightly, giving a whorled effect.

3-124. Circular whipped spider stitch.

108. Circular Woven Spider Stitch

Here is how to work a circular woven spider stitch (3-125).

a. Lay an uneven number of spokes—5, 7, or 9—all meeting at the same hole (1, 2, 3). Lay spokes A and B to the center point slightly above an imaginary horizontal line indicated by the dotted line. Divide the smaller segment into two, three, or four equal parts, and the larger segment into three, four, or five equal parts.

b. Needle up as near the center as possible between any two spokes, weave it over and under the spokes, working around the center (4). Pull through but only tight enough for the yarn to lie flat.

c. Continue weaving around the circle. After the first round the needle will go over the spokes that it went under on the previous round and under those that it went over; (5) shows a completed stitch.

109. Fan or Crescent Whipped Spider

This version of the whipped spider stitch represents only part of a circle (3-126). Gradual, subtle shading looks best.

a. Lay the spokes as illustrated (1, 2, or 3), depending on the shape being worked. Note that the outside ends of the spokes extend a bit beyond the outer line, as this line is difficult to cover.

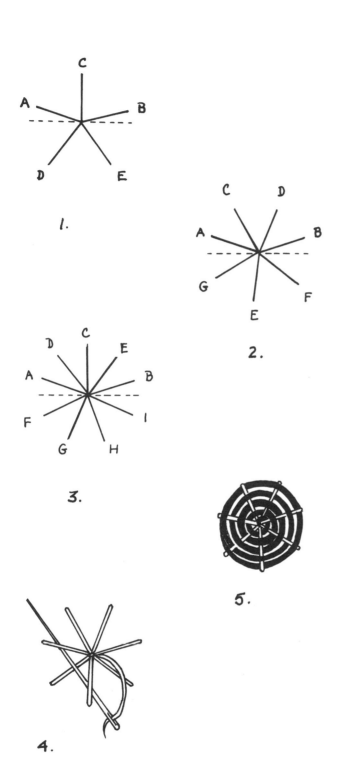

3-125. Circular woven spider stitch.

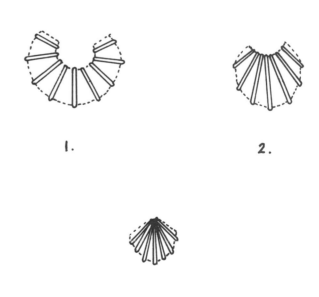

3-126. Fan or crescent whipped spider stitch.

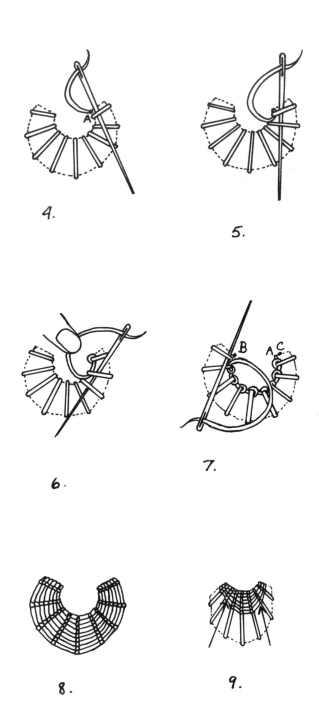

4.

5.

6.

7.

8.

9.

3-126. Fan or crescent whipped spider stitch.

b. Needle up at A on the inside line and on the right side of the motif. Hold the yarn back over the center of an imaginary circle (if it were completed) and slip the tapestry needle under the first spoke from right to left (4).

c. Pull through and hold the yarn back again.

d. Slip the needle under the first two bars (5).

e. Continue as in the circular spider, moving ahead one spoke each time and keeping the yarn taut under your thumb (6).

f. At end of row go under only the last spoke and take the needle down at B (7).

g. The yarn must be carried across the back to the right side to start the next row so that whipping will continue in the same direction. On the back slip the yarn under stitches or catch a few threads of the fabric and spread these carried-over threads out so that they will not make a lump on the back.

h. Needle up at C very close to A on the end line and repeat as for the first row, keeping the yarn taut and pushing back gently with the needle against the previous rows as the needle is slipped under the spokes for whipping.

i. As with the circular whipped spider, spread the whipped threads evenly on the spokes with the point of the blunt needle when bars are nearly filled. Then add the necessary number of rows to complete the spider. When finished, place the needle flat between bars and press and wiggle it back and forth to smooth the threads between the bars and to sharpen the ridges (8).

j. Since the end spokes on this type of spider are usually shorter than the center ones, it is necessary occasionally to skip wrapping the end spokes by going under two spokes when starting, continuing across as usual, and ending by going under the last two and taking the needle down on the end line. When omitting the end bars as described above, start and end in the same holes used for the previous row.

k. When the difference in the length of the spokes is very marked, as in (9), occasionally work a partial row by slipping the needle out from the under worked portion, working across the deepest portion, then ending by going down next to a spoke. These points are indicated by the two arrows (9). Sandwich these partial rows between complete ones, using your judgment as to where to begin and end as well as how often to use the partial rows.

110. Horizontal Whipped Spider Stitch

This variation of the spider is used to fill straight areas or areas that do not curve in only one direction. It is effective when used to fill the center portion of leaves. The approach is somewhat different (3-127).

a. Lay horizontal bars across the area, using double strands if the yarn is fairly fine and spacing them no more than 1/8" (3 mm) apart—slightly less when using a fine yarn. Make the bars taut and extend them a bit outside the lines (1).

b. With a tapestry needle come up at A, center point at one end of the area, using a single strand of yarn. Slip the needle under the first bar from right to left (2).

c. Pull through, hold the yarn back, and slip the needle under the first two bars (3).

d. Pull through. Place the needle under the first bar to hold it in position while yarn is pulled gently but firmly so that it will lie smoothly. This keeps the bar from being pulled out of line while the yarn is tightened around and between the bars (4). This same maneuver can be used when working any version of the whipped spider.

e. Continue working down the center of the area, with the needle going under two bars each time and tightening as described above as each bar is wrapped. Keep this line of yarn in the center of the shape.

f. Wrap the end bar, then take needle down at B, center bottom (5).

g. Needle up at C on outside line and very close to B. Turn the work and make the next line of whipping under the first row, following directions for the first row (6). Needle down at D very close to A.

h. Needle up at E on the opposite side of A, turn the work and make the next line of whipping on the other side of the center line of whipping. Needle will go down at F (7).

i. Continue working around the center portion, pushing back gently with needle against the center as needle is placed for whipping. Be careful to keep the horizontal bars straight, the yarn smooth between bars, and the whipping around the bars smooth by maintaining a firm, even tension while working.

j. As the narrow bottom bars are filled, drop them off and work along the outside lines as shown by the dots (7). The completed spider is shown in (8).

k. When the bars are almost filled, spread the whipping with the point of the tapestry needle, then add the amount needed to complete the spider. Press the needle flat between bars and wiggle it back and forth to sharpen the spider.

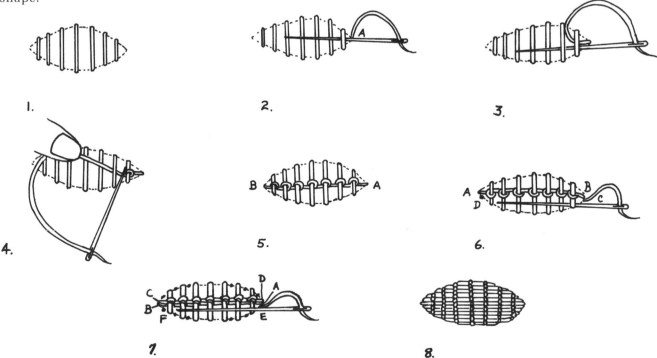

1.　　2.　　3.

4.　　5.　　6.

7.　　8.

3-127. Horizontal whipped spider stitch.

1.

2.

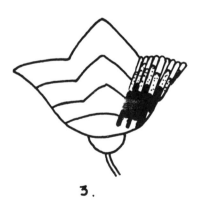

3.

3-128. Soft shading (long and short) stitch.

SOFT SHADING

111. Soft Shading (Long and Short Stitch)

The purpose of shading is to blend a number of values or shades of yarn together as subtly and as invisibly as possible—in much the same manner as the artist blends colors with brushstrokes. A good understanding of the technique involved will enable you to accomplish this blending with ease. Once you have mastered the mechanics of the procedure, there is practically no limit to the subjects that you can embroider effectively with shading. Some individual motifs illustrating shading in different situations are shown (C-9, C-10, C-11, C-12).

The most common term for this technique, long and short stitch, is misleading (3-128). As an example, if you are shading a motif with four values of a color, only the first step (which starts at a line) and the last step (which ends at a line) use long and short stitches (1, 4): the two values in between use stitches that are approximately the same length even though their placement is staggered in relation to each other (2,3).

The direction of the stitches in shading is of prime importance, since it will lead the eye of the observer, thus indicating or suggesting shape. Properly directed stitches can, for instance, emphasize the roundness of an object; improperly directed stitches can destroy the same illusion. In the case of an animal or bird the stitches should lie in the same direction in which the fur or feathers would lie. Otherwise the appearance of a strange, unbelievable creature would result. If a flower or motif starts from a stem, the stitches should converge at the point where it joins the stem (5). If a flower or motif is more or less rounded and has a center, the stitches should be directed toward this center (6). Stitches for a leaf may converge at the base where the leaf joins the stem (7) or lie in the direction normally taken by the side veins of a leaf (8).

A curved and undulating stitch direction will suggest motion and rhythm. If you are not sure just what direction the stitches should take, experiment with the shape on paper until you are satisfied. The direction lines should be marked lightly on your fabric, as indicated by the dotted lines (5, 6, 7, 8). These lines are an invaluable aid in keeping your stitches properly aligned as work progresses.

4.

Decide on the number of values to use in shading the motif, making sure to obtain sufficient contrast between the lightest and darkest values. Too little contrast will result in dull, uninteresting work. Another important consideration in choosing the number of values to use is the size of the space to be filled with the shading. Too many values crowded into a small space will necessitate the use of stitches that are too short for the smooth, flowing result that you want. On a large motif more values can be used, repeating a value more than once if the situation requires it, while on a small motif you may need to skip a value to obtain a satisfactory contrast.

After deciding on the number of values to use, divide your space equally, marking the divisions on the fabric, as indicated by the solid lines (5, 6, 7, 8), and making sure that they follow the outside contours of the motif that you are working. These spaces need not always be equal, since you might prefer light or darker values to predominate, depending on the situation. If you are new to the technique of shading, however, you would be wiser to use equal spacing until you feel comfortable with the technique.

5 .

7.

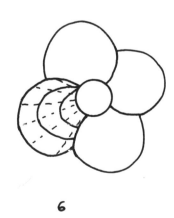

6

8.

SATIN STITCH EDGE METHOD

Work a row of split stitch around the outside edge of the motif, using the value of yarn that you planned on for that area. Start the first step of shading, working alternating long and short stitches. Bring the needle up at A on the first value-division line in the middle of the motif (9). With the needle in a vertical position, go down at B just outside the split stitch. (This line of split stitches will be entirely covered and will not be visible when the work is completed; its purpose is to help you achieve a smoother, neater edge.) This first stitch is a short stitch. Next to it and close enough so that no fabric shows between the stitches make a long stitch CD, coming up at C halfway into the second space and going down at D directly next to B. Alternate the long and short stitches, working to one side of the center. The other side will be worked after the first half is completed.

If you are working around a curve, you will occasionally need to work a compensating stitch EF, slipping the needle out from under the last stitch at E, then placing F next to the last stitch. Make a slightly longer short stitch, placing the inside end of this stitch directly next to the previous long stitch.

If you need a compensating stitch next to a short stitch, place the inside end directly in front of (not in the same hole as) the last stitch and the outside end alongside the last one. This maneuver helps you to change the direction of your stitches as you move around the curve. The inside ends of these compensating stitches occupy no new space, but the outer ends do. Change direction gradually, never suddenly.

When the stitching reaches one of the direction lines marked on the fabric, the last stitch should lie directly on that line. Watch these lines as you work so that you can anticipate any change you may need to make.

The difference in length between the long and the short stitches should be a minimum of 1/8" (3 mm), preferrably a bit longer, so that the values used in the various steps will blend smoothly together without showing lines at the transition points. Work the second side of the motif in the same way, starting in the center.

When all of the first value is completed, start the next value. With the staggered ends of the stitches facing you (9), come up through a short stitch at G, the third or fourth stitch from the right side (9), splitting through the yarn in the following manner. Split about one-third the way back into the stitch, bringing the needle from underneath at a very low angle to the fabric as it passes through the stitch (10). Since the needle and yarn of the new stitch pass through the first stitch over a space (rather than at one point, as would be the case if the needle were brought straight up through the stitch), no hole will be made. The first and second values will also blend together better than they would do if the stitch were split with the needle coming straight up through it. Pull through, laying the yarn on the fabric until the proper direction is established, using the directional guidelines marked on the fabric.

Go down on the second line at H (9). Use only sufficient tension for smoothness. If these stitches are pulled too tight, holes may form. Since these holes tend to destroy the beauty of soft shading, you want to do everything in your power to avoid them. You may sometimes find it necessary to split further back into a stitch in order to blend well. This can be done only when long enough stitches are used in the first step.

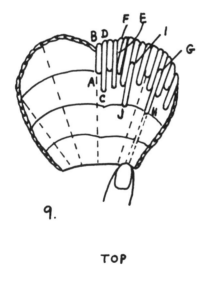

9.

TOP

SIDE VIEW

10.

Put in the number of stitches necessary to fill the space to the right of the stitch just made. If you split into a short stitch, bring the new stitch to the second line. If you split into a long stitch, bring the new stitch halfway into the third space (2). You may not need as many stitches as were made in the first step if the shape you are working narrows.

Jump three or four stitches to the left of stitch GH and make stitch IJ by splitting into a short stitch, lining the yarn up with the direction lines, and taking the needle down on the next line at J. Fill the space to the right of stitch IJ with the needed number of stitches to cover the fabric. Remember always to split the stitches as shown (10).

Continue working across the shape, jumping ahead a few stitches, lining up with the direction lines, and filling the spaces between. The purpose of this approach is to help you keep the stitches moving in the proper direction and to prevent you from putting in more stitches than are needed to cover the fabric. The latter will make the shading too thick and may obscure the ends of some stitches, thus breaking the staggered pattern for which you are striving.

Repeat this procedure for each value of yarn, always using the values in sequence. When working the last value, all stitches will end on the bottom line, thus using long and short stitches for the second time (4). Any steps after the first may be started at any point—in the middle or at the left or right side—the right side was used here only as an example.

After completing the second and any of the sub-sequent steps, hold your work at arm's length and look at it through half-closed eyes. There should be no definite line where any two values meet but rather a soft blending of the two. A stitch may sometimes be needed here or there to break an area where several stitches seem to form a line. It should be put in before proceeding to the next value.

BUTTONHOLE STITCH EDGE METHOD

A second method that utilizes a buttonhole edge offers the stitcher an alternate interesting edge for shaded motifs. The only difference lies in the first step. The work is begun on the left side of the motif—the right side for left-handers (11). Direction lines and value divisions should be marked on the fabric as with the first method. On the first stitch only do not go through the loop (this eliminates the hook made by the buttonhole projecting over the edge), ending with the yarn coming up on the outside line (11). Make the stitch lengths alternately long and short, still using the buttonhole stitch. For short stitches the needle should go down on the first value-division line, and for long ones it should go down halfway into the second space (12). The stitches must be placed close together so that no fabric shows between them. The second step of shading will be more successful if these stitches are close enough. If compensating stitches are needed to change direction, use the same methods described above. Stitches should line up with direction lines when the work reaches these lines. Subsequent steps are identical with those described in the first method.

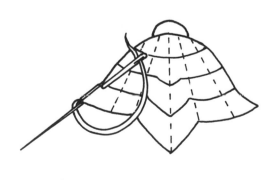

11.

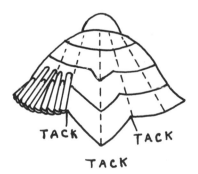

TACK   TACK

TACK

12.

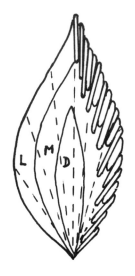

13.

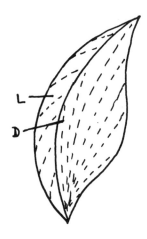

14.

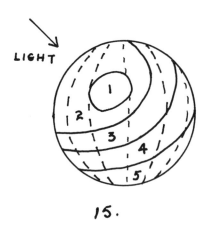

15.

16.

Different values of one hue may be used in soft shading, but a more interesting effect is often achieved by using more than one hue. Analogous colors blend well together, and green is effectively worked into any color. If your aim is to blend the two hues together subtly, use the same value when changing from one hue to another. If you want to create the effect of a sudden and abrupt change, exaggerate the points at which the stitches are split, splitting further back into alternate stitches in order to achieve this result.

Whenever possible, it is better to work from a wider area toward a narrow one, since it is easier to drop off and use fewer stitches while still achieving a subtle blending of values than it is to add stitches and maintain a satisfactory blending. When working the first step in either method, it may seem that you are using too much space for the first value. This situation will automatically correct itself in the following stages, since part of each stitch is lost when it is split.

When you wish to suggest a cup-shaped petal in a flower, the entire outside portion should be worked in a light value, then a medium value, and the darkest value in the center portion (13). Follow the stitch direction shown (13). When stitching this shape, it is usually best to start working the last or darkest value at the outer part of the petal, making a stitch first on one side, then on the other, then down the center, filling the center area as you work toward the base. You will often have to use your judgment as to the placement of some stitches, always working for a good blending of values. If a petal or leaf has a folded or turned-over edge, this portion should be light, with the area under the fold appearing darker and shadowed (14).

When shading a round object, it is generally wise to select a light source and mark the highlight, stitching direction lines and value divisions (15). Note that these lines are curved. By working in this manner you will enhance the feeling of roundness, creating more depth and dimension in your work. The placement of stitches at the bottom and along one side is shown in (16). These side stitches are almost parallel to the side, with the bottom end of the stitch carried over the split stitch and tucked in slightly under it. Once you establish the direction in which you are working, continue to work in this direction. If some of the working yarn is left when you are ready to change values, bring it to the top of the work out of your way rather than finishing and cutting it off. It can then be pulled to the back, slipped under the stitching, and used where needed.

If one petal lies over another (17), work split stitch around the edge of at least the overlying portion of the petal, even when using a buttonhole edge. This part of the petal should be light, with the area directly under the edge shadowed and darker. This placement of light against dark gives separation to the petals. Curving stitch-direction lines are shown in (18).

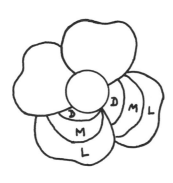

17.

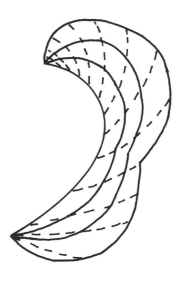

18.

Color

Color is exciting and alive with movement. It is also very personal and individual. Color should be a source of pleasure and enjoyment to the eyes and to the senses. Since we are constantly surrounded by color and since it is such a great influence on many aspects of our lives, we tend to take it for granted. Beautiful colors abound in nature, offering us many ideas for color schemes. We are exposed to color in the decoration of our homes, in the clothes we wear, in the books and magazines we read, in the stores where we shop, and in the food we eat. Color can actually vibrate and induce an emotional response in people, varying from one of calmness, caused by blues and greens, to one of excitement, produced by reds, oranges, and purples. We have all developed color preferences through our personal associations and experiences with particular hues. These are reflected in our color selections when buying clothing and home furnishings.

Individuals with a natural sense of color have more confidence in their ability to work with it and thus need less guidance than those with a less well-developed feeling for it. This latter group is often hesitant when confronted with a situation involving color selection. The best way to overcome this reluctance is to learn a few basic facts about color, then to jump in feet first and experiment. We learn by doing. If your first few efforts are not absolute perfection, the world will not come to an end. With each experience something new is learned, and, as you progress, it becomes easier, more fun, and more challenging. The pleasure of accomplishment and self-assurance is your reward.

TERMINOLOGY

When color is discussed, it is inevitable that specific terms be used. By studying these words, and referring back to them from time to time you will familiarize yourself with their proper usage. Simple definitions of some commonly used terms are as follows.

Hue means color and identifies it—i.e., red.

The intensity of a color refers to its brightness. It decreases as a color becomes duller.

Value refers to the relative lightness or darkness of a color (in relation to black and white).

Primary colors are red, yellow, and blue. They are equidistant on the color wheel. All other colors are derived from them.

Secondary colors are orange, green, and violet. They lie between the primaries.

Intermediate or tertiary colors fall between the primaries and the secondaries. This group includes colors such as blue-violet and yellow-green.

Complementary colors are opposite each other on the color wheel.

Analogous colors lie next to each other on the color wheel and are thus closely related.

A tint is made by adding white to a color.

A shade is made by adding black to a color.

Warm colors are psychologically associated with sunlight—i.e., red and yellow; cool colors are suggested by watery elements—i.e., blue and green.

C-2. Sampler of buttonhole stitch, many of its variations, and other looped stitches.

C-1. Sampler of chain stitch and many of its variations.

C-3. Sampler #1 of flat stitches.

C-4. Sampler #2 of flat stitches.

C-6. Sampler of couching and laid stitches.

C-5. Sampler of knotted stitches.

C-7. Sampler of filler stitches.

C-10. Soft shading, worked in curving lines and shading from one hue into another.

C-8. Sampler of weaving stitches.

C-9. Soft shading in a flower, showing separation of petals.

C-11. Soft shading, creating shape, contour, and dimension through placement of color values and stitch direction.

C-12. Soft shading of fruit. C-14. Intermediate design sampler.

C-13. Basic design sampler.

C-15. Advanced design sampler.

C-16. The Enchanting Forest, designed and
worked by the author on blue British satin in wool,
D.M.C. embroidery floss, and Perle cotton. It
incorporates the techniques of crewel, stumpwork,
petit point, and whitework on Aida cloth.

C-18. Yoke of a dress, designed and worked by
Judith Gorbutt. Photograph by Sun Photo, Ann
Arbor, Mich.

C-17. Cornucopia, a design adapted from a transfer and worked by the author.

C-20. Family coat of arms, worked by Gloria
Stirrat, photograph by Benyas Kaufman.

C-19. Vanity bench, designed and worked by
Paula Bidwell, photograph by Benyas Kaufman.

C-21. Bell pull, designed by the author and
worked by Zabel Arakalian.

C-23. Great blue heron, adapted from Audubon
print and designed by the author.

C-22. Chair, worked by Louise Schwab.

C-24. Blouse, designed and worked by Louise
Schwab in Perle cotton.

C-25. Fish, symbol of the Cape Cod Chapter of E.G.A., shaded with satin filler by the author.

C-27. Purse, based on intermediate design sampler; blouse, worked by the author in D.M.C. embroidery floss; pendant, worked in silk on velvet by the author.

C-26. Scroll, designed and worked by the author.

C-28. Color wheel. Primary colors are joined by heavy lines, secondary colors by solid lines, and complementary colors by dotted lines.

HARMONY

Color harmony is essential to a successful embroidery or composition. It is accomplished through an overall balance among hues, intensities, and values. A color may be affected by the other hues that surround it, either within a motif or in the background. To prove this to yourself, cut out several shapes from a piece of blue construction paper and paste them on red, yellow, purple, and orange sheets. Observe how the blue looks different on different background colors and how the blue and the orange intensify each other, since they are complementary colors. Try the same experiment with other colors.

BALANCE

Another important factor in the creation of a successful design is the balanced distribution of all its colors, whether dominant or secondary. One aspect of color balance is the repetition of a given color. It is very difficult to use a color only once.

4-1. The triangular method of balancing colors.

A color can dominate by virtue of its value, its intensity, its degree of contrast with the background, or its size or position. A very bright, intense color should not be selected for a dominant role, as it will overbalance the design, diverting attention from the overall effect. More muted tones of the same color should be used in dominant roles, with the brighter, more intense hues worked sparingly as highlights or accents. This will produce a greater impact, due to the contrast between the two levels of intensity. The intensity of the bright color will be diminished because of the smaller quantity used, and small, bright accents will add sparkle and interest to the composition. Darker shades should be used at the bottom of the design to balance it and to give it weight.

A dependable system for color placement relies on the triangle method (4-1). It is possible to establish triangular patterns visually rather than by drawing them on the design worksheet. In your first experiments, however, you may find it easier to draw in these triangles to ensure a good color balance.

When working with a small design and a limited number of elements, it is necessary to limit the number of colors used, and you may not be able to use the triangular method. When this occurs, place the main color, then locate a second spot of the same color in a diagonal position from the first. Entire leaves or parts of leaves can be stitched in a color other than green, and filler stitches and the small elements of the design offer further opportunities for balancing colors.

CONTRAST

Sufficient contrast among values and intensities is just as necessary as is color balance. The artistic term "chiaroscuro" is defined by the dictionary as "the treatment of light and dark parts of a pictorial work of art." A piece of embroidery that lacks sufficient contrast may be technically perfect but will never have the impact or appeal of a piece that does exhibit good contrast between the light and dark values. This same factor of contrast is necessary for separating and defining various areas of a motif or design element.

SELECTION

Some general factors need to be considered when selecting colors for a piece of embroidery. These include the colors in the area in which the article will be used, the color preferences of the individual who will be using the article, and the color of the background fabric. This latter point is important, because the colors chosen must complement and contrast with the background in order to silhouette the design.

An informal approach to color selection for an embroidery is to use a color scheme from a favorite painting, fabric, magazine illustration, or wallpaper pattern. Start a file of such resources for future reference. These color schemes have been worked out by experts who are knowledgeable in the use of color. A more technical approach involves the use of the color wheel and conventional color schemes.

A primary color scheme uses red, yellow, and blue. It is direct and unsophisticated, a favorite of children. Since many crewel yarns are manufactured in muted shades, the primary color scheme can be used without creating too bright a result.

The triad scheme is similar to the primary scheme in that the key color is an intense primary, while the other two colors are muted tones of the other two primaries.

A complementary color scheme utilizes colors opposite each other on the color wheel. These colors are often found in nature and, when used together, enhance, strengthen, and emphasize each other without causing the hues to change.

A variation of the complementary scheme is the split-complementary scheme. In this case the main color is used with the two hues lying on either side of its complement.

Analogous color schemes use colors that are next to each other on the color wheel. These colors have an emotional quality and are most effective when the main color is a primary or secondary.

Monochromatic color harmony is created by us-ing different values and intensities of the same hue. In spite of the fact that some teachers use this color plan with beginning students, it is considered by many authorities to be an advanced technique, since its success depends on achieving sufficient contrast among and balance of the various values and intensities.

In most designs, unless they involve repeats, there is one motif or area that acts as the focal point. Place the main or dominant color there. That area will also display the strongest contrast of values and intensities. Place the dominant color in at least one other area—and in a third, if possible. Then place and balance the hues for the secondary areas. Greens play a subordinate role in crewel, acting as a foil for the other colors. They should therefore be more or less subdued. Even large pieces of embroidery are usually more effective when the number of colors is somewhat limited.

On your first attempts at planning colors for a design a helpful method is to place a sheet of tracing paper over the design worksheet and, using crayons, watercolor pencils, or some other coloring medium, to arrange and balance the colors. The outlines need not be transferred to this sheet. Try several different color schemes or arrangements until you are satisfied. This plan can then be colored on the design worksheet and used as a guide for stitching.

CHECKPOINTS

Some helpful checkpoints include the following.

1. Is each color (including the greens) balanced throughout the design?

2. Does any one spot or area "hit you in the eye?"

3. Are the various hues, values, and intensities balanced?

4. Is the design "held down" by sufficiently dark values?

5. In each motif, element, or area are the values placed so as to define and separate the different parts?

Design

Design is a means of self-expression, a personal statement that illustrates the forces that have the greatest meaning for an individual, whether they be movement, rhythm, or a love of nature.

There are varying degrees of creativity among embroiders just as among all people. Some are contented to work designs created by others. Others start in the first category but progress to the point that they subconsciously want to create their own designs. But these people often hesitate because they are unsure of their ability to design and uncertain about where and how to begin. This group is by far the largest. The smallest group is composed of people who are compelled to do their own designing and who need little guidance because of their natural creative ability.

Designs should be suited to the purpose for which they are made and to the specific shape involved. A particular design may fit perfectly into one size and shape but be completely wrong for a different size and shape. We think of creating a design to fill a space. But this is not altogether true, for the unembroidered area or negative space is just as important as the part that is stitched. Too little negative space causes the design to appear crowded and detracts from the individual elements, while too much space results in a vacant appearance.

SOURCES

Books illustrating crewel designs from the past offer a wealth of inspiration and ideas, both for shapes and forms and for design arrangements. Not all the designs are good ones, but for this very reason they are good study material that you should use as a learning tool.

A wide range of design styles developed through the years, from the Elizabethan through the Stuart, Jacobean, William and Mary, Queen Anne, and early American periods. Some span two periods and include elements of both. Designers in the twentieth century should not feel obligated to follow any one particular style of the past: instead we should consider what appeals to us personally and create in our own individual style.

Ideas and inspiration for design are everywhere. Once you become aware of design itself, you will view your surroundings from a new perspective. For example, you will notice how leaves grow from a stem; you will consider the shape of a particular flower in relation to its use as a design motif. You will look at a seed pod or at one small portion of it in terms of its design possibilities instead of its function as a whole. You will find yourself noticing designs in fabrics, wallpaper, upholstery, placemats, paper napkins, towels, illustrations in magazines, greeting cards, gift-wrapping paper, dishes, and vases. Museums offer much food for thought in regard to design. The list of possibilities is endless. What is important is that you view everything with its design potential in mind. A new, exciting world is waiting to be discovered. Everyone who aspires to creativity should start a notebook of sketches and pictures—of leaf and flower shapes, which can be used in their original form, adapted, simplified, or stylized; of arrangements and forms; of patterns made by lines (often found in photographs); of geometric arrangements; and of simple leaf and flower shapes that can be joined together for border designs.

5-1. *Basic sampler illustrating design principles,*
worked on upholstery linen with Appleton yarn.

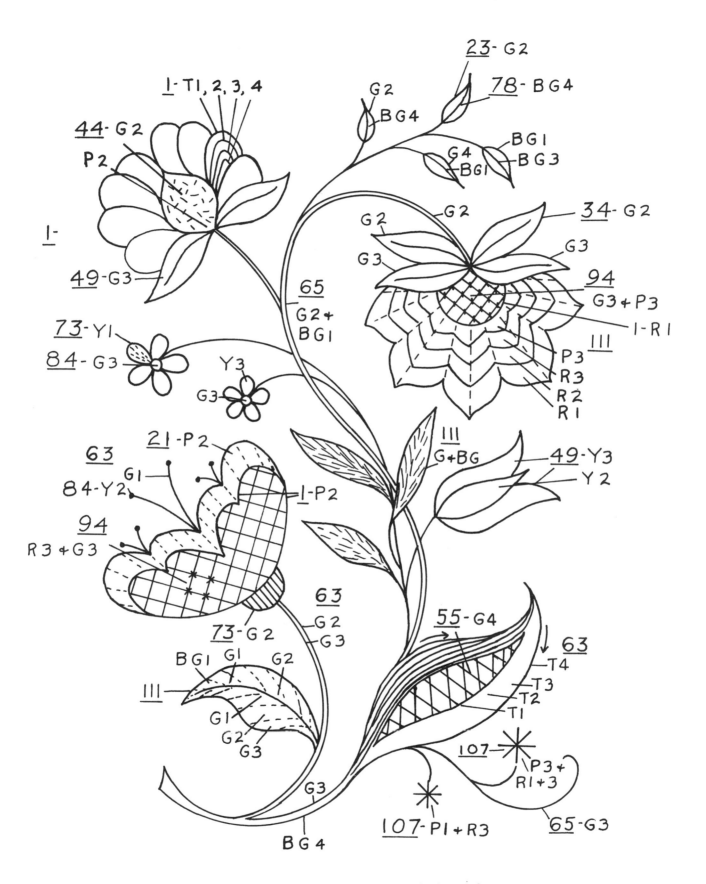

5-2. Line drawing and guide for the basic design sampler.

Color Key
R 1, 2, 3—rose wool
T 1, 2, 3, 4—turquoise wool
P 1, 2, 3—purple wool
Y 1, 2, 3—yellow wool
G 1, 2, 3, 4—green wool
BG 1, 2, 3, 4—blue-green wool
The lowest number indicates the lightest value.

Stitch Key
  1 chain stitch
 21 close buttonhole stitch
 23 detached buttonhole bar stitch
 34 closed fly stitch
 44 seed stitch
 49 fishbone stitch
 55 open herringbone stitch
 63 outline stitch
 65 whipped outline stitch
 73 satin stitch
 78 straight stitch
 84 French knot stitch
 94 simple trellis stitch
107 circular whipped spider stitch
111 soft shading stitch

1. Upper-left motif—work outer edge of petals first in a light value, then add successive rows in value sequence to fill each petal. Fill center with seed stitch.

2. Lower-left motif—work close buttonhole, then the filler, then a row of chain around entire filler.

3. Upper-right motif—shade using buttonhole edge, tacking at both outside and inside points. Work filler, then chain around filler. Work leaves last.

4. Middle-right flower—work side petals first. When center vein ends, continue with slanting satin stitches, maintaining same slant and spacing. Then work center petal.

5. Lower-right—work open herringbone first. Work outline stitch on upper side of leaf from base to tip, using partial lines as needed, and work lower side from tip to base (see arrows).

6. Leaves in center are shaded from light blue-green into dark green, starting at tip. They may also be worked in any leaf stitch. The remainder is either self-explanatory or the sequence is not important. Stems can be worked last so that all elements join together smoothly.

5-3. Intermediate sampler illustrating design principles, worked on black chino cloth with Appleton yarn, D.M.C. embroidery floss and #8 Perle cotton. It can be used in many ways, since the design is multidirectional.

5-4. Line drawing and guide for the intermediate design sampler.

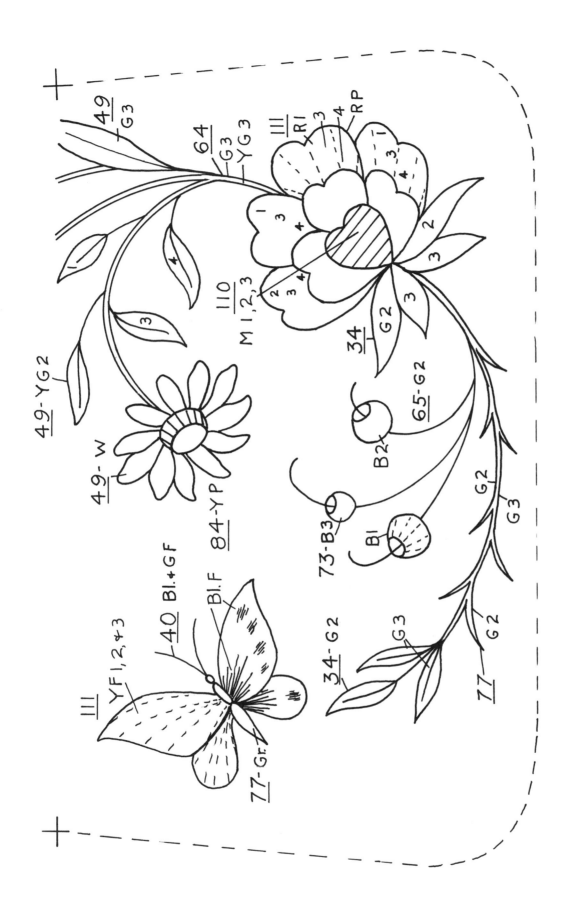

49
‾‾
G3

64
‾‾
G3
YG3

III
‾‾
R1

4
3
RP
3
1

49-YG2

1
3
4

4

110
‾‾‾
M1,2,3

3

2
3
4

3

2
3

2

3

34
‾‾
G2

49-W

65-G2

B2

84-YP

B1.F

B1

40 Bl.+GF

73-B3

G2

G3

III
‾‾ YF1,2,+3

34- G2

G3

77
‾‾
G2

77- Gr.

Color Key
R 1, 2, 3, 4—rose wool
RP—rose Perle
B 1, 2, 3, 4—blue wool
BF—blue floss
YG 1, 2, 3, 4—yellow-green wool
G 1, 2, 3, 4—green wool
GP—green Perle
GF—green floss
M 1, 2, 3—mauve wool
MP—mauve Perle
MF—mauve floss
Y 2, 3, 4—yellow wool
YP—yellow Perle
YF 1, 2, 3—yellow floss
W—white wool
WF—white floss
BlF—black floss
Gr—gray wool
The lowest number indicates the lightest value.

Stitch Key
　1　chain stitch
　7　detached chain stitch
　18　twisted chain stitch
　21　close buttonhole stitch
　34　closed fly stitch
　35　serrated fly stitch
　36　open fly stitch
　40　whipped back stitch
　49　fishbone stitch
　63　outline stitch
　64　stem stitch
　65　whipped outline stitch
　73　satin stitch
　77　split stitch
　81　bullion knot stitch
　83　coral knot stitch
　84　French knot stitch
107　circular whipped spider stitch
109　fan spider stitch
110　horizontal spider stitch
111　soft shading stitch

1. Butterfly—shade, using one strand of yellow floss and three values. Do not use split stitch on edge of wings, as they will appear thinner without it. Antennae are in whipped back stitch, one strand of black whipped with one of green floss. Head is satin stitch in gray; body is split stitch in gray.

2. White shaded flower—shade the petals with one strand of floss, working from white into light blue. The center is curved bullion knots, using one strand of mauve and one of blue floss threaded together in the needle.

3. Shaded rose flower—shade outer petals using buttonhole edge. Work buttonhole over ridge made by buttonhole of shading, catching no fabric, one stitch for each previous one, using medium rose Perle or silk buttonhole twist. French knots on inner petals are worked with one strand of wool and one of Perle threaded together in needle. Shade by changing values from light outside to dark inside.

4. Mauve flower—use two rows of coral knot in #8 Perle to outline petals. For fishbone petals work the two in back first, the two outside ones next, then the center one, using either split stitch along edges and working stitches over it or raised fishbone for depth.

5. Match crosses on either side of design to give the complete design. The rest of the design is self-explanatory.

5-5. Advanced sampler illustrating design principles, worked on linen twill with Appleton yarn.

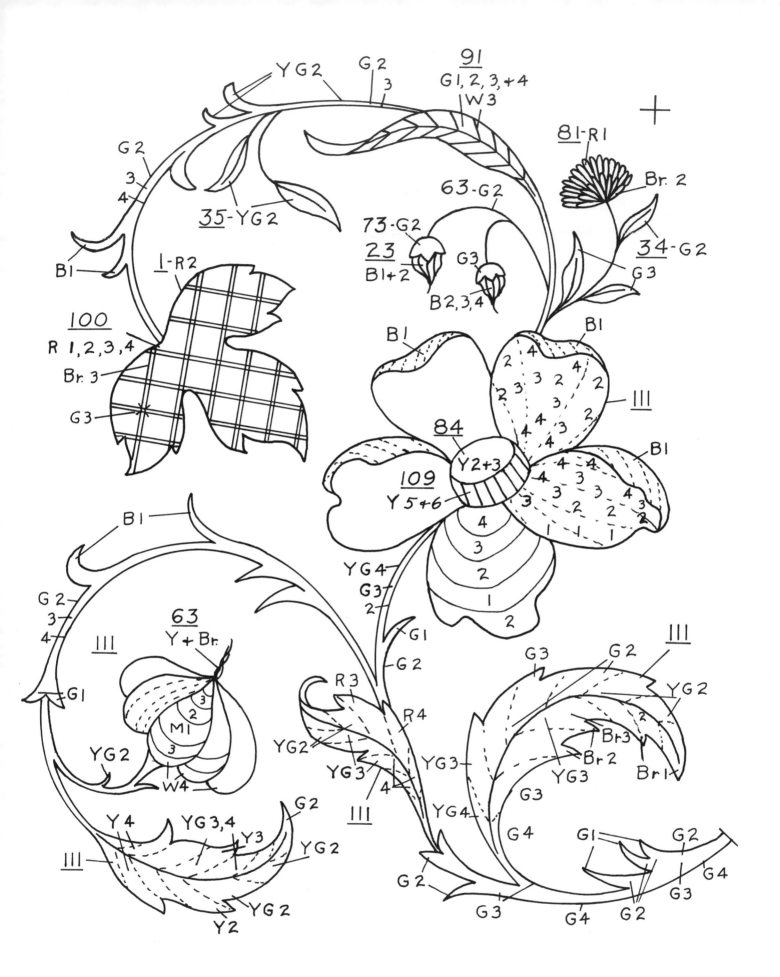

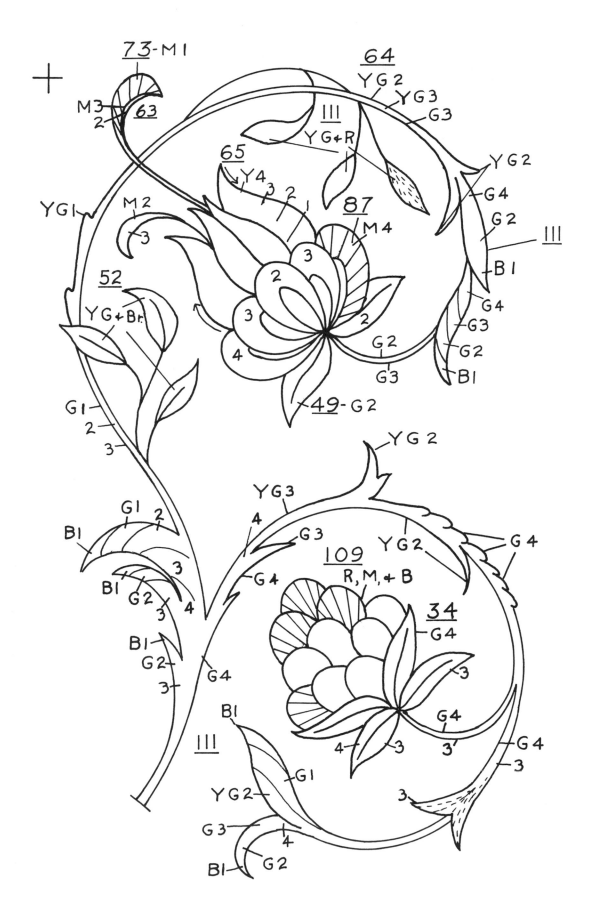

5-6. Line drawing and guide for the advanced design sampler.

Color Key

B 1, 2, 3, 4—blue wool
R 1, 2, 3, 4—rose wool
M 1, 2, 3, 4—mauve wool
W 3, 4—wine wool
Y 1, 2, 3, 4,—yellow wool
Br 1, 2, 3—brown wool
G 1, 2, 3, 4—green wool
YG 1, 2, 3, 4—yellow-green wool
The lowest number indicates the lightest value.

Stitch Key

  1 chain stitch
23 twisted detached buttonhole stitch
34 closed fly stitch
35 serrated fly stitch
49 fishbone stitch
52 shaded fishbone stitch
63 outline stitch
64 stem stitch
65 whipped outline stitch
73 satin stitch
81 bullion knot stitch
84 French knot stitch
87 raised knot stitch
91 couched leaf stitch
100 satin filler stitch
109 fan or crescent spider stitch
111 soft shading stitch

1. The scrolling stems are worked entirely in stem stitch, blending from one color or value into the next as you end with one and bring new thread up for the first step of the next stitch. At some points yellow-green is blended into green, and vice versa. The leaflike projections from the stems are shaded, then blended into the stem stitch.

2. Large blue flower—work split stitch around edges of petals that lie underneath and shade these first. Follow direction lines and number values as marked on direction sheet. Then do the other petals that lie on top. The turned-over edges of petals are worked in slanting satin stitch over split stitch on both edges of turnovers. Center of flower is worked last.

3. Upper-right motif—work rows of whipped outline stitch from base to tip on the lower half and from tip to base on the upper half of the motif. Follow direction lines and use partial lines as needed.

4. Where stem joins the upper-left motif slip in a few deep rose stitches. On lower-left motif work in a few stitches of mauve where it joins the stem.

5. On lower-right motif work outermost section first, then the two that overlap it, and so on. Start with light rose shading a bit deeper, then into mauve in outer areas, changing to slightly darker tones as you work toward the base. Some are shaded into grayed blue, and some from mauve into blue. Use your own judgment or follow the picture to place these colors and values. The spiders in this situation are rather challenging and tricky but produce a most unusual result. If you prefer, they can be worked in close buttonhole instead.

6. Match cross and diagonal line on stem at bottom to make complete design.

PRINCIPLES

There are no hard-and-fast rules for designing, but there are certain basic principles that apply to all art forms.

Proportion encompasses the relationship of sizes to each other and of the design to the background. All the elements should not be the same size (unless the design is a repeat), but the differences of space arrangement should be in harmony.

In order for a design to appear unified, all its parts should look as if they belong together and should complement each other. This does not mean that they must be alike. They can and should vary in order to prevent monotony.

All lines and shapes should blend harmoniously.

Contrast, whether in color, tone, line, shape, or texture, is a necessary element for the creation of an interesting design.

Lines must be used to connect shapes and elements of a design. At the same time they fulfill other functions. They create motion, rhythm, and change. They lead the eye through the design. Curved lines suggest grace and movement; diagonals are dynamic and indicate strength; horizontals produce a feeling of calmness, restfulness, and space; verticals suggest dignity.

Balance refers to the total effect of all the components of the design.

The dominant center of interest or focal point can be established by the size, shape, position, line, structure, color, and/or treatment of an element or specific area of the design. It should not generally be dead-center but in the locations indicated by the X marks in relation to the center point of the composition (5-7).

PUTTING A DESIGN TOGETHER

Design is a trial-and-error process; it does not happen automatically. There are many approaches to creating a design. The following is the method that I have found to be the most satisfactory.

1. Decide on what you want to design, its size, shape, and the use to be made of the finished article. Put the outline of this shape on tracing paper. This will be your worksheet.

2. Select the elements that you wish to include in your design. Check them against the principles of proportion and unity.

3. Put all the elements on another piece of tracing paper and cut around them, leaving a bit of paper beyond the outer lines.

4. On the worksheet sketch in the basic lines of the design. If you are making a symmetrical design, fold the shape in half or quarters first, then draw the basic lines.

5. Select an element for the focal point and position it. Locate the larger supplementary elements, trying them in various positions and at different angles and moving them around until they are balanced (5-8).

6. Slip these elements underneath the worksheet in the proper position and trace them onto the sheet in the selected locations.

7. Place the smaller secondary elements in the same manner, filling open spaces and balancing all the components. Keep in mind the basic principles, checking your design against them as you work. When you are satisfied with the arrangement, slip these elements in position under the worksheet and trace them.

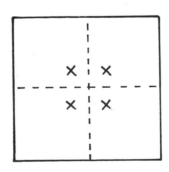

5-7. Ideal placement of the focal point or dominant center of interest.

5-8. Order of placement for the focal point and other main elements of a design.

8. At this point take a critical look at the design and decide whether this particular composition is successful. Viewing it in a mirror often reveals errors that are not otherwise apparent. Make any needed adjustments. Check to see that all aspects of the design are arranged in such a way that they hold the eye within the design and do not lead it away from the composition. Placing animals, birds, insects, or people so that they look into the design helps to achieve this. Stems should not point directly to a corner.

9. If the worksheet was folded for a symmetrical design, trace the design onto the other half or quarters of the sheet.

10. Put the design on the wall where you can look at it briefly from time to time and can view it from a distance. A quick glance at an odd moment will often help you to see a needed change that is not evident when you study it in depth. This is a form of subconscious self-criticism and is helpful in attaining self-confidence.

11. Do not be in a hurry to put the design on fabric. Think about it carefully and go back to it several times, giving yourself plenty of time for evaluation.

12. Before putting the design on fabric make a color plan and decide on the stitches, as these two factors can influence the placement of motifs to some degree.

ENLARGING AND REDUCING A DESIGN

Here is a reliable method for enlarging a design, especially for those who are not adept at drawing.

1. Draw lines 1/4" (6 mm) apart in both directions over the drawing. I prefer to do this on a sheet of tracing paper and to place this over the original.

2. Draw lines 1/2" (12 mm) apart in both directions on another sheet of paper. This will make the new drawing twice the size as the original one.

3. Make the new drawing, using the lines and squares as guidelines. If you want the new drawing to be half again as large as the original, make the squares 3/8" (9 mm).

4. This same method can be used to reduce the size of the original by reversing the procedure and making the second drawing over smaller squares.

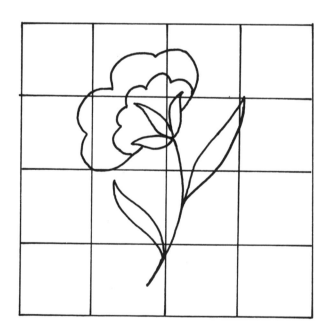

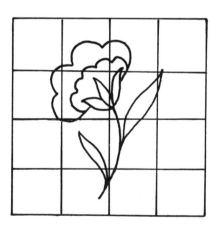

1.

2.

5-9. Methods of enlarging or reducing a design.

TRANSFERRING DESIGNS TO FABRIC

A wide variety of designs can be purchased as iron-on transfers. To transfer them to fabric, first brush off any loose particles of transfer ink and trim off any parts that you do not want to include. Turn the transfer shiny side down, center it on the fabric, and pin smoothly in place on two or three sides. With a moderately hot iron go over the entire design. Do not push the iron back and forth. Peek under a corner to see if the design is transferring properly. Test the degree of heat needed with the discarded cut-off parts. Some fabrics will accept the transfer better if the fabric is first warmed with the iron.

For your own designs or any designs that are not in transfer form an Eberhard Hectograph transfer pencil can be used to go over the design on tracing paper. Remember to reverse the design. This reverse pattern is then treated as a hot-iron transfer. Experiment to determine how hot the iron must be to satisfactorily transfer the design without scorching the fabric. Some transfer pencils will make more than one copy from a single tracing.

Dressmaker's carbon, which can be purchased from any sewing center, is used by some individuals, though in my experience it does not always transfer well. A more satisfactory carbon is graphite carbon, which can be purchased in large office- and art-supply stores. It is a gray, thin, semi-translucent paper as opposed to the commonly used opaque carbon paper. Another kind is called Saral and comes in a roll of five colors.

To transfer a design using graphite carbon, first smooth the fabric. Center the design and pin it in place. Slip the carbon between the two, carbon side down, and, working on a hard surface, carefully trace around the design with a slightly blunt hard pencil. Experiment first to determine the amount of pressure needed. If you wish to make the design permanent, go over the lines with a fine-point laundry marker, working from the center out and being careful not to smudge the ink while it is still wet. I prefer to work with the graphite lines rather than the hard, dark, permanent ones and to reinforce them as I work if they fade too much. This method is satisfactory in most cases.

Still another way to transfer a design is the pricking method. Using a needle with the eye embedded in a cork or an eraser and with the design reverse side up over a piece of felt or cardboard, prick the outlines, placing holes close together. Make a small pad of rolled-up felt and, using light-colored powdered chalk for dark fabric and powdered charcoal for light fabric, rub lightly over the design in a circular motion. Check by lifting a corner to make sure that the lines are clear. Lift the paper off carefully. The design can be gone over with a laundry marker or with a fine brush and white or blue watercolor. Experiment to find the proper proportion of paint to water.

DESIGN ELEMENTS

The following pages offer an assortment of design elements and leaves in varying sizes to be used in making up your own designs. They can and should be supplemented by some of your own. Choose the elements that you like best and follow the directions given in this section for putting a design together. The old art of cutting folded sheets of paper results in surprisingly lovely designs ranging from the simplest to the most intricate.

5-10. A repeat border design.

129

1.

2.

3.

4.

5-11. *Stem lines and arrangements of design elements.*

5.

5-12. Symmetrical folded cut-paper designs.

134

Washing, Blocking, and Finishing

PRESSING

A piece of embroidery can be pressed as the work progresses if needed. Press only on the back with the right side face down on a turkish towel. Press with a good steam iron, pulling fabric only straight across or up and down with the grain. Some people claim that this should not be done, but I have never had any adverse results from it.

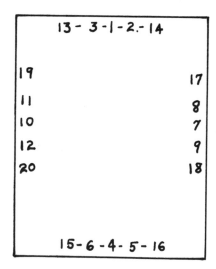

6-1. The numerical sequence for placing pushpins when blocking.

WASHING

When the embroidery is completed, washing and blocking will freshen, brighten, and fluff up the wool, giving the work new dimensions. You must first be certain that all materials are colorfast. If you are not sure, test samples of the materials used, going through the same procedure that you will use when washing and blocking except that they need not be stretched. Wash in cool water and a gentle soap or detergent. Squeeze the suds through the fabric thoroughly and rinse until all soap is removed. Roll in a towel, squeezing out excess moisture.

BLOCKING

A blocking board can be made from a piece of Celotex wallboard or a ceiling tile that will take pushpins. Cover it with muslin or percale, which can be marked with horizontal and vertical lines about 2″ (5 cm) apart, using an indelible marker. Or it can be covered with gingham—colorfast, of course—which already has built-in lines.

Straighten the fabric and place it face up on the blocking board. Using aluminum pushpins, a good grade of strong thumbtacks, preferably rustproof, put in pins 1, 2, and 3 (6-1). Hold this spot with one hand and pull straight down to the center bottom, putting in pins 4, 5, and 6. Pull evenly across the center from both sides and put in pins 7, 8, and 9.

Hold that spot firmly and stretch to the opposite side for pins 10, 11, and 12. Stretch up and out toward the corner for pins 13 and 14; stretch down and toward the corner for 15 and 16. Repeat for 17 and 18 and for 19 and 20. Continue in the same manner until the entire piece is stretched, always pulling as taut as possible and working from the center toward the corners. Some fabrics, such as twill, become quite stiff when wet. After it has dried for about an hour, the fabric will relax and loosen up a bit. The piece can then be restretched, one side at a time, if necessary. This second stretching will remove any wrinkles left the first time. Leave in a horizontal position for about 24 hours. The embroidery is then ready to be finished or framed for hanging (6-2).

Upsom board, available at lumberyards, is a good material to use for mounting a piece that is to be framed. Use board 3/8" to 1/4" (1 cm) thick and staple or lace the finished piece to it, working the centers first and stretching as you mount toward the corners and out from the center. The embroidery should be isolated from the Upsom board with acid-free paper or muslin before mounting. If the piece needs to be cleaned, it is easily removed, rewashed, blocked, and reframed.

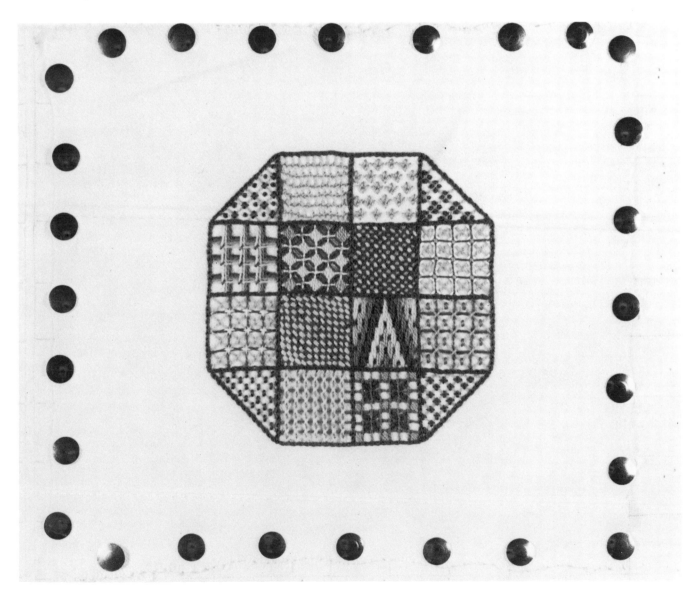

6-2. *A piece of embroidery on the blocking board.*

FINISHING

Here is how to finish a piece, in this case a purse (6-3, 6-4).

1. Cut 1/2″ (6 mm) outside the line of the design for a seam allowance.

2. Cut a piece of the fabric (1) for the inside front of the purse, adding 1/2″ (6 mm) on all sides. Cut a strip of fabric 2″ (5 cm) wide and long enough to fit around the two sides and bottom of piece 1.

3. Cut a piece of lining to fit piece 1, another the size of the strip, and a third to fit piece 2.

4. Cut two pieces of the heaviest Pellon interfacing, one the size of the embroidered fabric with the seam allowance and one to fit just inside the seam line (shown by the dotted line). Center and sew the smaller one to the larger one, then sew the complete interfacing to the wrong side of the embroidered fabric along the seam line. Trim the interfacing close to the stitching. Repeat for piece 1.

5. Stitch the strip of lining to the strip of fabric, wrong sides together, making a 3/8″ (8 mm) seam. Stitch the lined strip to piece 1, right sides together, from A to B, turning in and hemming the ends of the strip. Trim the seam and clip the curves at the bottom corners. Sew lining to piece 1 along the top edge, right sides together. Turn to the inside and slip-stitch closely over the seam made by the strip. If you wish to use cording or braid in the seam, insert it as the seam is made.

6. Sew the unstitched side of the strip to piece 2 from A to B, right sides together. Trim the seam and clip corners.

7. Turn the remaining piece of lining and of the purse flap under along the seam line. Turn the purse inside out and slip-stitch the lining over the seam line.

8. Sew snaps of Velcro fasteners (shown by the circles) for closure.

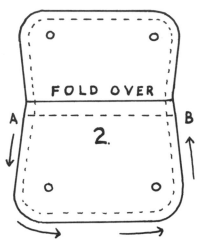

6-3. *The outlay of the purse.*

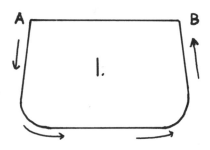

6-4. *The front piece of the purse.*

Bibliography

Bath, Virginia Churchill, *Embroidery Masterworks*, Regnery, 1972.

Birren, Faber, *Principles of Color*, Van Nostrand Reinhold, 1969.

Bucher, Jo, *Complete Guide to Embroidery Stitches and Crewel*, Meredith Corporation, 1971.

Chevreul, M. E., *Principles of Harmony and Contrast of Colors*, Reinhold, 1967.

Davis, Mildred J., *The Art of Crewel Embroidery*, Crown, 1962.

Endacott, Violet M., *Design in Embroidery*, Bonanza, 1963.

Enthoven, Jacqueline, *The Stitches of Creative Embroidery*, Van Nostrand Reinhold, 1964.

Rubi, Christian, *Cut Paper Silhouettes and Stencils*, Van Nostrand Reinhold, 1970.

Stovi, Gunter, *American Folk Art Painting*, published by author.

Whyte, Kathleen, *Design in Embroidery*, Batsford, 1969.

Wilson, Erica, *The Embroidery Book*, Scribners, 1973.

Index of Stitches

See the numbers referred to in chapter 3 for a description of these stitches.

Index